PRAISE FOR "WOKE"

"I know of no other book that explains so clearly, with so lively a pen, and with such economy the various intellectual currents that are now disturbing our cultural peace. What is even rarer is that the author grinds no axes, treating both sides of the culture wars with thoughtful charity and a deeply Christian intelligence. 'Woke' has important things to say and it does so in a highly readable manner."

— **Nigel Biggar, Ph.D.**, Regius Professor Emeritus of Moral Theology, University of Oxford

"There is no substitute for common sense and Stackhouse brims with it as this book testifies. It is a dangerous time. All the more reason to value this book."

— **Stanley Hauerwas, Ph.D.**, Gilbert T. Rowe Professor Emeritus of Divinity and Law, Duke University

WOKE

AN EVANGELICAL GUIDE TO POSTMODERNISM, LIBERALISM, CRITICAL RACE THEORY, AND MORE

JOHN G. STACKHOUSE, Jr.

THINKBETTER Media

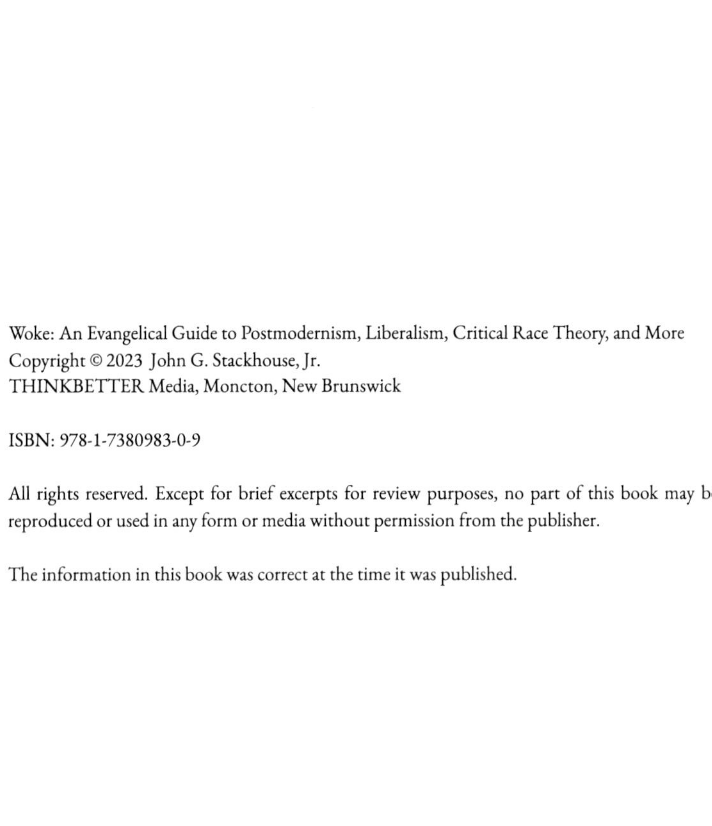

Woke: An Evangelical Guide to Postmodernism, Liberalism, Critical Race Theory, and More
Copyright © 2023 John G. Stackhouse, Jr.
THINKBETTER Media, Moncton, New Brunswick

ISBN: 978-1-7380983-0-9

All rights reserved. Except for brief excerpts for review purposes, no part of this book may be reproduced or used in any form or media without permission from the publisher.

The information in this book was correct at the time it was published.

Cover Design: Sarah-Jane Britton
Interior Layout: Jonathan Puddle

to SJ,
who has awakened me
to so much

CONTENTS

Introduction

This book is doomed.

It is doomed, that is, if readers come to it expecting a comprehensive treatment of every subject it addresses. Whole books, some of them good, have taken up just one or two of the many topics this booklet addresses: postmodernity, Critical Theory, liberalism, socialism, communism, multiculturalism, diversity, equity, and inclusion (DEI), Critical Race Theory, anti-racism, and political correctness.

It is doomed also if readers come to it expecting a comprehensive presentation of the Christian Story, the Christian world-and-life view, fundamental Christian ethics, and the implications of all of that for life and witness today. Whole books of mine, some of them good, have taken up one or two of those topics as well.

What this small volume can do, however, is provide a brief introduction and response to the culture of "woke" for those professionals, pastors, parents, and other people too busy or otherwise disinclined to undertake a deeper study. My aim is to help Christians who don't have time to read a lot of books but who earnestly want to think better about these issues we all face—so that we can understand and respond to those issues with clarity, charity, vigour, and effectiveness.

If you read this book with that important, but modest, objective, then it ought to be worth your while.

Woke: An Evangelical Guide is in two parts. The first introduces and explains a range of key ideas—from postmodernity to political correctness—all of which help define aspects of woke culture. My strong sense is that these terms are often, even usually, used wrongly, and especially by people who ought to know better: preachers, pundits, and other purveyors of public opinion. In my experience, in fact, anyone who is not a scholar in a relevant field who uses any word starting with "postmodern" almost certainly misuses it. And all around us people are spouting off about Critical Race Theory, "cultural Marxism," and the like while clearly being clueless about these ideas. So we will take time to do what Kong-zi (the sage we Westerners know as "Confucius") said was the first step in any good thinking: the "rectification of names"—or, as we professors tend to say, defining our terms. The second part of the book offers Christian reflection on each of these cultural elements, resulting in practical advice to parents, students, pastors, educators, policymakers, and any other concerned Christian citizens. We want to think better in order to live better.

The first name we must rectify, of course, is the term "*woke*" itself. Woke refers to being awake, and specifically to whether Black Americans in the 1940s were awake to the systemic patterns of racial discrimination they were still experiencing, long after the abolition of slavery and the Civil War. Black Americans encouraged one another to "stay woke" to the injustices they were suffering and to refuse to accept them as simply an unavoidable and unchangeable part of life. In that original positive spirit, I stand in the long tradition of evangelicals who desire to keep our eyes and ears open to what is really happening to us and around us—and particularly to those of our neighbours who suffer injustice.

I appreciate that *woke* more recently has been used ironically and pejoratively by people on the cultural and political right to mock what they see to be self-righteous excesses of progressive zeal. So I will use *woke* in multiple ways throughout this booklet, sometimes in ways that progressives may not enjoy and sometimes in ways that conservatives may find challenging.

I should also define evangelical. I've written a lot on the question of defining this term, and readers are directed to *Evangelicalism: A Very Short Introduction* (Oxford, 2022) for a proper treatment. For now, I just mean vital, observant Protestant Christianity, the style of Protestantism between conservative ("maintain the tradition") and liberal ("open to changing nearly anything under the 'Christian' brand"). I mean the kind of Christianity now exploding in China, Korea, India, Latin America, sub-Saharan Africa, and even Iran. I do not mean to restrict it to "white American nationalism," as I recognize many readers might wonder if that's what I mean to do. I mean the kind of Christianity fostered in the eighteenth century by the Wesleys, George Whitefield, Lady Huntingdon, and Jonathan Edwards and in our own time by organizations ranging from World Vision and the Salvation Army to the World Evangelical Alliance and the International Fellowship of Evangelical Students.

This little book has emerged from my journalism, public lectures, teaching, and books over the last decade or so. Those used to my more academic writing may notice I have maintained here a journalistic tone, right down to the omission of citations, merely noting sources in passing—as journalists get to do. I trust that that style will frustrate only the occasional reader (such as myself: I love footnotes) and will free everyone else to read through it at a pace convenient to you.

Thanks very much, then, to my Crandall University colleague Dr. Diandra Singh, who has worked with Critical Race Theory and whose personal experience as an Indo-Canadian woman has brought sober perspective to the parts of the book she helpfully critiqued. Thanks to the versatile Jonathan Puddle for crucial production and marketing assistance in launching this new publishing venture of ThinkBetter Media. And thanks to Sarah-Jane Britton, partner with me in ThinkBetter Media, among other projects (let the reader understand), who inspires the author to, on so many fronts, think better.

Part One

Chapter One

Postmodernity

When I was a student in the 1970s and 1980s, *postmodernity* was still cool. Then it became conventional. Then boring—and even irritating when someone breathlessly announced that she had just discovered it and wanted to celebrate it, or perhaps warn us about it. But now?

Now it's significant to everybody, because postmodernity is everywhere.

A book this short cannot possibly do academic justice to such interesting and paradoxical phenomena. But since pundits from Jordan Peterson to the late Tim Keller, as well as a host of lesser lights, have been offering their takes on these complex matters, let's plunge in and see what's what—especially since a lot of popular Christian speakers lump in all things "woke" with postmodernity.

And they shouldn't.

The "post-" in "postmodernity" tells us that the word means simply "what comes after the modern." What comes after the modern, it turns out, is both much more of the same, in intensified and extended form (hence the term *hyper*modernity) and also something importantly different (hence the term *post*modernity).

So what is the "modern" after which comes postmodernity?

By "modern," most historians mean the culture experienced by the West since the seventeenth century or so and now by much of the rest of the world. When speaking of the "postmodern" experience, most scholars refer to two main respects: *fragmentation* and *doubt*. Let's compare those two postmodern qualities with the modern qualities of *differentiation* and *confidence*.

Starting with the *modern*, then, sociologists give us the term *differentiation*, the process by which various social sectors and social roles become progressively distinct and separate from each other. Family life, education, health care, politics, recreation, religion—all of these become separate spheres with their own values, their own objectives, and usually even their own spaces, uniforms, and jargons.

A modern person gets out of bed in his pyjamas on a Monday morning and quickly changes into different clothes to exercise at the nearby gym. After a workout, breakfast, and a shower, he changes his appearance again and goes to a different place to work. After work, he likely changes his look once more to go out with friends for dinner. And then he might change clothes again to participate in a Bible study, or attend a support group, or assist a local charity. Once home, he changes once more (notice the way we easily use the word "changes") to be with his domestic partner(s).

Modern people feel the strain of playing all these different roles in all these different places according to all these different values. The changes throughout the day take a toll. The basic concern of the gym for physical fitness is absurd in the workplace, where what matters is financial productivity. Out for the evening, though, prioritizing bodily conditioning or fiscal advantage will quickly lose one friends and disrupt whatever leisure-time activity one is undertaking. And at home, one had better prioritize loving relationship over exercise, stock-trading, or texting acquaintances!

Modern people, as I say, feel the strain of feeling pulled apart into these socially differentiated sectors. *Post*modern people are therefore, in this respect, *hyper*modern people. They experience all this social diversity—but they don't feel the strain. They just *are* different people in different situations, flickering from one fragment of personality to another as the day goes on and their contexts and communities change. The fully postmodern person has little or no core identity, and no abiding and guiding value-system other than maximizing what one has decided on one's own is The Good Life.

The second key quality of the postmodern experience is *doubt*. Modern people enjoyed the confidence that the smart people were steadily improving and expanding our knowledge. We didn't have all the answers yet, and maybe we never would. But the Big Explanations furnished by those smart people—of science, of history, of religion, of politics—were giving all of us a better and better handle on the world, a handle we then applied in various technologies to make the world do what we wanted.

This confidence postmoderns have lost.

We have endured a century and more of Big Stories told to justify this or that regime—whether the British Empire, or the Bolshevik Revolution, or Nazi nationalism, or American hegemony, or socialist utopia, or globalized capitalism. After this century of propaganda and advertisement, scandal and disgrace, conspiracies and cartels, meltdowns and explosions, and a stream of broken promises, we've all had enough.

No longer do we trust anyone—*anyone*—who represents power to have our best interests at heart.

"Hello, I'm from the government, and I'm here to help you."

Right.

We don't trust politicians. We don't trust CEOs. We don't trust journalists, or clergy, or military leaders, or police officers. We don't even trust physicians and scientists. Anyone might be bought. Systems serve themselves, not those they use and abuse. And anyone who has been promoted by a system to a position of prominence has been promoted *in the interest of the system*, not according to some abstract code of merit or ethical excellence. No influential person suddenly shows up in our lives focused on helping us, but on helping themselves and the system they represent.

Or so a postmodern person believes.

Furthermore, we each see things from our own particular point of view. There is no neutral knowledge. We perceive the world according to what we understand to be our own interests and in accord with the outlook of our peer group of the moment (whether we're at home, or at work, or at the club, or at church). That's just life. Who can possibly know anything important for certain, objectively, truly?

Postmoderns aren't cynics or paranoiacs. They don't believe that every single person is up to something nefarious. They don't believe—as lots of Christian critics in particular say they do—that *there is no truth* at all. Postmoderns don't deny that there is truth (or, as some pundits tiresomely put it, "absolute truth"). What postmoderns have lost is *the confidence that we can know* that we know the truth. Instead of that confidence, we have suspicion that anyone who claims to know The Answer is about to rope us into a self-serving scheme.

So when a stranger comes calling, or shows up in the media, and says, "Hi, there! I've got the Grand Account, the Total Explanation, that will solve all problems!" the postmodern reflex is incredulity toward all such metanarratives (in the phrasing of Jean-François Lyotard), all such Big Stories—which is to say, "You claim you've got it all figured out and you want me to believe it? *I doubt it.*"

We are all postmoderns now—at least in respect to this abiding dubiety about all such claims. We jump with suspicion when the doorbell rings or when an unfamiliar name shows up on our cell phone display. We snort when a nicely dressed, smooth-talking character in a movie says, "How can I help you?" since we're pretty sure he'll turn out to be the serial killer.

This combination of fragmentation and doubt is the fog in which we now live our lives. And the postmodern architecture of our cities nicely articulates both these themes in jumbles of disparate styles arranged according to no overarching, universal aesthetic.

That's where the term "postmodern" first surfaced, actually: in buildings whose design took a bit of this (say, the curved back of a Chippendale couch), blew it up to a huge size, rendered it in concrete, and stuck it on the top of an otherwise conventional modern skyscraper—as in one of the earliest famous postmodern buildings, the AT&T Building in New York (now "550 Madison"). Any suggestion that there was, or ought to be, a single governing architectural style was dismissed as preposterously arrogant. Instead, fragments of the past were to be joined to contemporary fabrics and shapes to create pastiches that, it was hoped, would be fresh and interesting.

But who could say for sure?

Welcome to postmodernity.

What, however, does all this talk about the postmodern experience have to do with Critical Race Theory, or liberal politics, or workplace initiatives in diversity, equity, and inclusion? How are all of these features of wokeness somehow to be blamed on postmodernity, as so many right-wing pundits claim?

Well, they mostly aren't.

And to make that point clear, let's now look at the "cultural Marxism" reputed to be behind so much that is dubious and even frightening in woke culture: Critical Theory.

Chapter Two
Critical Theory

Are you a cultural Marxist? Is he? Are they? How would you know?

The first chapter in this little book defined postmodernity, a form of society in which, I suggested, we all now currently reside.

Let's be clear, however, that I am not claiming that all of us all the time think as postmoderns. Engineers and physicians, at least on the job, think as heirs of the (modern) Enlightenment, while historians and social scientists think in terms of (modern) historical consciousness. Instead, I have argued that postmodernity is now common, even typical, in our society.

Outside certain domains and discourses (as academics would say) in which we still think as moderns, postmodernity is our mental and social environment. We go from place to place, group to group, and role to role throughout our days, weeks, and years displaying changing sets of character traits suitable for the occasion—fragments of ourselves we put together to fit this or that situation. And we typically doubt anyone who claims to tell the Big Story (the "metanarrative") that explains the world for fear that she is selling us a lie to get what she wants from us.

It turns out, however, that modern confidence hasn't just evaporated except, say, for the hard and applied sciences, such as physics and aeronautics. In fact, most of woke culture turns out to be persistently modern.

In journalistic explanations of current controversies over “cancel culture,” “Black Lives Matter,” “Critical Race Theory,” and the like, the philosophical school known as “Critical Theory” bobs up frequently. Critical Theory is sometimes depicted as an early form of postmodernism that gives rise to these other cultural developments.

But it isn’t. It’s modern.

Critical Theory refers to a group of twentieth-century German philosophers known as the Frankfurt School. The most famous among them are Max Horkheimer, Theodor Adorno, Herbert Marcuse, and Jürgen Habermas—the last of whom is, at the time of this writing, still productive in his 90s.

The “critical” in Critical Theory evokes Karl Marx’s famous dictum: “Philosophers have hitherto only interpreted the world in various ways; the point is to change it” (*Theses on Feuerbach*, 1845). Critical Theory draws on both philosophy and the social sciences in order to expose the true workings of modern life and to formulate a way toward a better future than the paths offered by communism, fascism, or democracy wedded to runaway capitalism.

Note, then, the small paradox. Critical Theorists have been successors to Marx in both their quest to unmask what’s really going on in society and in their intent to offer a better alternative. True, most of them were indebted to at least some of Marx's ideas, even though none can properly be called an orthodox Marxist. (Hegel, Heidegger, Freud, and other definitively non-Marxist thinkers loom large for one or more of the chief Critical Theorists.)

Unlike Marx, however, the Critical Theorists have not focused mostly on economic matters as the main engine of social change. And this is the crucial difference. They submitted everything in society to their philosophical and social scientific X-rays, from art to politics to religion. They viewed culture as important in itself, not merely as a function of financial forces. Most crucially, they don't see the way forward as inevitable class warfare, as Marxists do, but as a long process of democratic negotiation.

"Cultural Marxism" has been suggested as a term to describe (and to dismiss) this kind of thinking. This term is chiefly used, however, by people who don't understand Critical Theory but want to wield "cultural Marxism" as a stick with which to beat opponents to their political and cultural left. We're better off not using the term at all, since it is at least as wrong as it is right.

Everywhere the Critical Theorists have looked, people with power were exploiting people without it, often dressing up that exploitation in Big Stories of "the common good," or "the good of the nation," or "the good of humankind." In this sense, the Critical Theorists have been allies of the postmodernists as both groups think they see in all ideologies mere legitimations of unjust relationships.

Critical Theory is not, however, postmodern. It is modern in its confidence that truth can be found, if laboriously rather than easily read off the surface. ("Things aren't what they appear—but we can find out what's what, and change it" could be a slogan, in fact, for most modern philosophers.) Critical Theory, moreover, has also sought the one right way to live the Good Life, rather than despairing, as postmoderns do, of ever knowing for certain if anything is important or true or even helpful.

In short, Critical Theory is antiskeptical, while the postmodern outlook is deeply skeptical.

Paradoxically, democracy is therefore the best form of politics for both Critical Theory and for postmoderns, albeit in different respects. The Critical Theorists maintain a hope that if everyone enjoys and practices free speech, unconstrained by official ideology or the repression of major corporations, what is true and good will emerge into ever greater clarity and attractiveness. Indeed, Critical Theorists incline to what is nowadays often called a *progressive* politics precisely in that they believe that so long as the political sphere is truly open to rational discourse—without warping or silencing by powerful interests—and particularly if once-marginal voices are given platforms, individual and communal betterment will eventually be worked out in the extended conversations and transactions of a liberal (= "free") culture.

Postmodernists hold out no hope that we will all eventually agree on major values. The next best thing, in their view, is to secure as much liberty as possible for each person and community, while sticking together for certain common goods: security from external threats, internal order, basic logistics (roads, sewers), and the protection of fundamental human rights. Postmodernists thus typically opt for democracy, not because they are particularly hopeful of good results, but because the wide distribution of power across a wide electorate at least diffuses the threat of any one individual or community dominating another.

But just a second. I thought "liberals"—like these postmodernists and Critical Theorists—all yearn for a socialist state that would rob us of our freedom and our hard-earned money. I thought all these lefties want to dictate how everyone has to behave. And the final stop on this leftward line is communism.

Isn't that what one hears from the right these days? What about liberalism, and socialism, and communism? We shall consider those next.

Chapter Three

Liberalism, Socialism, and Communism

So what about those liberals—by which I mean, those socialists—by which I mean, those communists?

In this chapter, we'll look at a few terms everybody thinks he or she understands: liberalism, socialism, and communism.

Spoiler alert: most people don't, in fact, understand them. And we must.

It's true that the term "liberal" has undergone substantial definitional alterations over the last several centuries. But let's keep before us the basic etymological datum that "liberal" comes from *liber*, Latin for "free." In that light, we will see that mainstream North American political life since the American Revolution and Canadian Confederation has been almost entirely liberal, as it has also been in modern Britain, Australia, New Zealand, and beyond.

The political scientist Louis Hartz published an influential volume in 1955 called *The Liberal Tradition in America*. In it, he convincingly argues that American politics (and, I am saying, politics in Canada and other modern democracies also) ranges within the liberal part of the political spectrum. What is liberalism, thus understood? Respect for the freedom of the individual that entails the protection of basic human rights, the rule of law treating everyone equally, constitutional constraints on power, governance by elected officials, and so on.

Few of us today, or even in the last 60 years, would call for the divine right of kings or would like to be ruled by a charismatic priest or prophet. Not many of us advocate communism, or fascism, or governance by a military junta. If we consider the full spectrum of political options thrown up by history all around the world, all of ours are relatively close together. The real options on offer in modern countries are all *liberal* options—even as some people worry that storm clouds are gathering in Europe toward dictatorships, and Africa is rife with them.

Indeed, it makes more sense to think of our politics as contests among various forms of "conservative liberals" and various forms of "progressive liberals."

Conservatives want to keep most things the way they were—even if their vision of the past is distorted somewhat by nostalgia and self-interest. Change, if change there be, should come slowly and piecemeal.

Progressives want to change most things for the better, even if their vision of the future is distorted somewhat by utopianism and, yes, self-interest. Change, at least on certain subjects that seem obvious to them, should come ASAP.

Both sides are very happy to employ the state to get certain things done. Don't believe the "small government versus big government" talk as if that distinguishes the right from the left. It doesn't.

The American federal government has dramatically increased under both Republican and Democratic administrations with remarkable consistency. And we haven't seen much self-restraint by Liberal or Conservative governors up here in Canada, either. Where the two sides differ is mostly over *what issues* the state should govern, and thus *where* the government should extend its reach—not *if* it should at all.

Conservatives are happy for the government to constrain people's liberty on issues of, say, abortion and euthanasia. Progressives want the government to constrain people's liberty on issues of, say, workplace safety and wealth distribution. (The history of which issues are championed by which side is a complex and interesting one. Progressives nowadays promote legalized marijuana, but they used to support Prohibition. Progressives nowadays promote sexual license for virtually any adult, but they used to support eugenics and the forced sterilization of "deplorables" of various sorts. This complexity also means that progressive liberals and conservative liberals in one nation may vote in different ways to their counterparts in another nation.)

Paradoxically, both conservative liberals and progressive liberals should, and normally do, favour antitrust intervention against monopolies and cartels in the marketplace. Why? Because such concentrations of economic power prevent the working of a truly free market. And only the government is a big enough player to stand up to Standard Oil . . . or Microsoft . . . or Wal-Mart.

This is a crucial point, worth repeating. Conservative liberals and progressive liberals *both* want a big (enough) government to do what they want done, and much of what they want done can be accomplished only by a big (enough) government. The difference between them, therefore, is about *what* they want done. And some things they *both* want done can be done only by a big (enough) government: national defense, for instance—even as there can be a wide range of opinions about what national defense should entail.

Socialism is an extension of this logic. Left to itself, the market can, and often does, produce dysfunctional disparities of power such that the market itself can no longer function as a free arena of innovation. (Think of attempting an online search for something Google doesn't want you to find. Imagine trying to buy something Amazon doesn't want to sell you. Now think of attempting to start up a company to compete with Google or Amazon.)

Socialism responds to this concern about market dominance—this *liberal* concern *shared* by conservatives and progressives alike—by having the state intervene. The state here, in a liberal democratic situation, is empowered by each citizen casting a vote to appoint those who will govern. It is this democratically elected and democratically responsible state that is charged not only with reining in or even breaking up anti-liberal situations (conservatives, even libertarians, might agree with such action), but also with permanently administering sectors of society too important to be left to the cold machinations of the marketplace.

Socialism has dozens of varieties. Essentially, however, socialism says that the major forms of power in a society must be kept in the hands of all citizens through democratically elected institutions. Only responsible government can be counted on to act for the common good. Left to the law of the jungle, power will inevitably concentrate in the hands of a single class (capitalists, those who own large things and large amounts) who are free to advantage themselves to the disadvantage of everyone else. And we don't want such people in charge of, say, major utilities, or public education, or mass transit, or health care.

Communism is therefore one variety of socialism. Communism means governmental control of pretty much everything in public life, whether commercial concerns, from industries to stores, public services, from power companies to hospitals, or cultural institutions, from schools to studios. But communism is the most extreme form of socialism. To insinuate that all socialism is communism, or even that it tends that way, is nastily ridiculous—although opponents have been summoning up the spectre of communism against all forms of socialism for a century or more. To tar socialism with the brush of communism is as wrong as saying that all capitalists are enthusiastic about child labour, the abolition of unions, and the wholesale removal of workplace and environmental safety standards. *Some* capitalists are just that rapacious, yes. But it would be slanderous to say, or even imply, that *all* of them are—or even that capitalism inevitably ends up in such extremes.

Socialist governments of various hues, we might observe, have dominated much of western European politics since the Second World War. They have also formed the government of most Canadian provinces at least once since the Co-operative Commonwealth Federation (now the New Democratic Party) was formed in 1932. And not once has communism ever emerged in any of these countries as a serious contemporary option.

It also must be recognized that the competitive pressures and open possibilities of a free market have proven vastly superior to all competitive economic alternatives (including socialism and communism) in producing wealth and fostering innovation. No serious person is entirely against capitalist economics nowadays. Even the Nordic states, long held up as bastions of social democracy, rely on capitalist economies at least in part.

Moreover, we all recognize that governments themselves are inevitably corrupt to at least some extent. Many governments are so corrupt as to be dominated by the wealthy and are thus unresponsive to the electorate, and few governments are not deeply swayed by the preferences of the powerful. So socialism isn't a magical solution somehow devoid of the stains of human frailty and sin. Furthermore, governmental oversight, we must realistically allow, sometimes makes things worse and sometimes makes things better, but it never makes anything perfectly better.

"Capitalism vs. Socialism" is therefore a gross oversimplification of our current political and economic choices. Our actual arguments are over *more* or *less* government supervision of *this* or *that* sector of our society in order to produce the best possible outcome in a world compromised by selfish power.

Let's tie all this back to Critical Theory and postmodernism. In any given case, either of those outlooks might opt for a socialist process or a free-market one, however the democratic conversation among all citizens eventually comes out. Critical Theory's basic politics are *hopefully* democratic, while postmodern politics (at least in theory) would be *skeptically* democratic. Their economics, likewise, could be either socialist or capitalist in regard to any particular sector: utilities, say, or elementary schools, or social media, or medical clinics.

Now we come to a nagging question. If democracy is consistent with both postmodernity and Critical Theory, and a contest between "pure" socialism and "pure" capitalism isn't the issue in real economic discussions today, why are we hearing so much nowadays about the clearly antidemocratic "cancel culture"—the latest anti-liberal variety of "political correctness"—as if it is a symptom of increasing socialism . . . and even communism?

One answer is that people are just confused—even people who assume the task of explaining these things to other people! This is partly true, and I trust this booklet will help us sort out what are and what are not actual links among these various terms and issues.

Another answer is that lacking a power structure willing to address concerns of injustice (originating with the sexual exploitation of female film stars, before branching out to the hiring practices of fast-food chains and offshore companies), "woke" social media participants were encouraged to boycott (punish) those individuals or companies that the justice system, government, and the market all had refused to regulate or examine. Such campaigns necessarily tend toward polarization and the resulting oversimplification of options.

Yet another answer is that something is going on that does indeed draw on both postmodernism and Critical Theory, while other things are going on, much more broadly, that make every conversation about difference much more difficult. We have yet to talk about Critical Race Theory, anti-racism, and political correctness.

Before we do, however, we should look at the apparently more benign versions of progressivism showing up not only in electoral politics but in our schools and workplaces. For better and for worse, it's time to consider diversity, equity, and inclusion.

Chapter Four

Diversity, Equity, and Inclusion

Remember multiculturalism?

If you're a Canadian or an Australian, you have multiculturalism as a formal responsibility of a federal government department (or "ministry," as we British types prefer to say). If you're an avid reader of the political press, you know that several European heads of state pronounced multiculturalism dead a decade ago (British prime minister David Cameron and German chancellor Angela Merkel among them). And if you're any younger than a millennial, you likely don't know what I'm talking about.

Say the word "diversity," however, and little explosions detonate in everyone's mind.

Some people hear it and complain about how much things have changed since they were kids. Others hear it and bristle at how much things *haven't* changed and *should*. Still others hear the word and rejoice in the varieties of cultures their children experience at school, in the wider array of restaurants nearby, and in the brave immigrants they have met at work who escaped from difficult situations to come here and take on new challenges as they contribute enthusiastically to our common life.

Bigger explosions go off, however, when I say, "Critical Race Theory." Or "anti-racism." "Diversity, equality, and inclusivity"—often called "diversity, equity, and inclusion"— is the new slogan of contemporary schools and workplaces. "CRT" is in the shouts of those both for and against drastic changes in society. And "anti-racism" is the new crusade for justice in many quarters.

It's time for us to think better about all three of these linked, but different, ideologies.

Here we'll consider "diversity, equity, and inclusion" (DEI) to sort out what is actually common-sensical about it all, what must be critically regarded as a campaign, and what ought to be embraced as true courtesy to our fellows. (The scandalized among us might bad-temperedly rearrange the order to spell out "D-I-E." In some places, the acronym is EDI. And my alma mater, The University of Chicago, settles for just "diversity and inclusion.")

We won't spend time critiquing the likes of popular authors Robin DiAngelo, Ibram Kendi, or Voddie Baucham, none of whom strike me as requiring serious attention here. But we will look at the basic ideas in these conversations to get past common oversimplifications—which are rife in this discourse—to what really matters.

Let's turn, then, to "diversity, equality, and inclusivity." I will refer to "inclusivity" rather than the also-popular "inclusion" and "equality" instead of "equity" to maintain a helpful parallel usage. (I will acknowledge for word-lovers that "equity" and "equality" can sometimes mean importantly different things. In this language-game, however, I don't think they consistently do.)

These terms go back in the scholarly literature more than forty years. The ethical and political impetus goes back much further: to abolitionism, suffragism, and other nineteenth-century campaigns for the rights and dignity of all people. The DEI surge, therefore, is simply the latest wave of the surge for justice for and, even more, full acceptance of the previously marginalized or oppressed, the surge that has transformed western societies particularly since the 1960s.

Over these decades, these terms have settled in their definitions. One can see in these three conjoined elements three parallel affirmations. I will reverse the order to show how they build.

Inclusivity: All lives matter.

Equality: All lives matter equally.

Diversity: Each life matters.

Let's include everyone, leaving no one out. We used to leave people out. Lots of people. Depending on the "we" and where "in" and "out" were, we left out women, and children, and poor folk, and foreigners, and non-ethnic-majority people, and sexual minorities. Inclusivity is the impulse of embrace. Let's exclude no one. All are welcome.

Let's value everyone equally, regarding no one as more important, or more human, or more sacred than anyone else. We used to observe strict hierarchies, and those higher up could command, exploit, and just plain lord it over those lower down. In the United States Constitution, enslaved people were determined to have 3/5ths the voting value of a free person. Earlier still, men, women, and children were valued differently when the law demanded economic compensation to the family for manslaughter—the so-called *wergild*, or "man-price." Only recently in some countries, and to this day not in all, husbands are subject to prosecution for striking or raping their wives. Equality is the motive of levelling. Let's respect everyone with equal dignity.

And let's endorse individual difference. If multiculturalism tends to emphasize variety of communities, diversity tends to emphasize variety of particular persons. We used to prefer conformity, and we often insisted on uniformity. Diversity is, at least, the motive of acceptance, and, at best, celebration. You be you and that'll be okay with the rest of us, and we might even celebrate your differences.

Whence come these values that are so quickly, even insistently, espoused nowadays by corporations, schools, and media alike?

As a historian of contemporary culture who has at least a nodding acquaintance with matters of religion and society, I feel compelled to point to Christianity's huge and fundamental influence on western culture. This is where we find the origins of anything like "diversity, equity, and inclusion."

The Hebrew Scriptures, which we Christians have appropriated as our Old Testament, put Israel in the centre of the story, sure. That sounds ethnocentric in the extreme. But Israel occupies that position as a "light to the nations," as a living example to everyone else of "life with Yhwh." (I spell the name of God given to Moses at the burning bush this way to indicate both that it is God's chosen name, an actual name and not a title—such as "the Lord"—and also that we don't know how it was pronounced, since vowels came much later than consonants in ancient Hebrew.)

The early prophets make clear that Israel is not especially noble, wise, holy, or otherwise worthy of Yhwh's attention and affection. Quite the contrary. Israel serves as a kind of encouraging lesson, and it's a lesson with a punchline. "If God can do all this with and through even the likes of Israel, imagine what God could do for you!"

Israel was warned against any religious compromise with the gods of other nations and likewise against political alliances with other kings. Israel was to worship and trust Yhwh alone. But Israel was also commanded to treat any foreigners living among them with full dignity. Diversity, equality, and inclusivity are evident in the Old Testament from Genesis to Malachi.

The New Testament ramped up this message even more. The boundaries of the people of God expanded to a global identity as the universal church of Jesus Christ. No longer bound to a land and an ethnicity, God's chosen are "everyone who believes." When Paul says, "In Christ there is neither Jew nor Gentile, male nor female, slave nor free" (Gal. 3:28), he is setting out a contextualized parallel to diversity, equity, and inclusion.

Biblical eschatology in both Testaments, furthermore, points to a messianic kingdom in which diversity, equality, and inclusivity are evident in abundance. The kings of the earth bring the glories of the nations to the worship of God in the New Jerusalem. In the age to come, human beings do not suddenly transform into generic lookalikes. We remain who we were—as individuals and as nations—even as we become the very best versions of ourselves as fitting inhabitants of a glorious new earth.

Christian societies that have formed since New Testament times have actualized these ideals, if only fitfully, slowly, and painfully. It took a very long time, yes, for even something as grotesquely wicked as slavery to be outlawed. It took a very long time, yes, for women to become even just officially equal with men. It took a very long time for race to be discredited as a construct, let alone removed as a social principle. It took a very long time for poverty to be seen as something other than culpable moral failure.

And the marks of these evils remain in Christian-majority countries—even in some Christian churches and families. Worse, Christian terms and even the Christian Scriptures themselves have been perverted and continue to be bent into the service of vicious principles and practices.

Moreover, the Enlightenment—which, let's be clear, included atheistic resenters of Christianity (such as Diderot) but also enthusiastic proponents of the faith (such as Wesley)—took up some of these principles with fresh vigour to inspire many people, not all of whom were inclined to look to the Church for cultural and political reform. And secularized versions of these ideals continue today to animate the quest for justice and the acceptance of each and all. It certainly isn't only Christians who care about diversity, equity, and inclusion. In fact, many contemporary champions of these ideals look askance at the Christian church as a resistant enemy in this campaign.

Still, it remains historically pertinent to note that it was not in other cultures—cultures older and in some ways wiser than the West—that slavery was abolished, universal suffrage was instituted, and diversity, equity, and inclusion have been championed. It has been in the West, whose fundamental cultural current has been Christian.

The main point I want to make here, however, is not one of Christian apologetics, but of Christian politics. Christians ought to look on campaigns for DEI with at least prima facie approval. We *like* diversity, equality, and inclusivity. We have been preaching and practicing these values for centuries—however partially and even hypocritically we have done so. These are our values, too.

Alas, sometimes proponents of DEI seem to go too far. We'll pick up that point shortly.

Other people think that the DEI values and agenda are evident in Critical Race Theory (CRT). So they support CRT as a helpful approach to the accurate analysis of modern life. Still other people, however, fear that CRT instead is a destructive tool wielded by woke extremists against our society, and particularly against our schools and against our children.

Next, then, let's examine Critical Race Theory.

CHAPTER FIVE

CRITICAL RACE THEORY

Critical Race Theory (CRT) sounds like Critical Theory (CT) by no mere coincidence. The former clearly derives from the latter.

Let's recall, then, that Critical Theory subjects society both past and the present to philosophical and social scientific analysis, looking below the surfaces to expose the real mechanisms, and machinations, below. Critical Theory expects to find that the stronger tend to exploit and oppress the weaker, that privilege fights to keep its prerogatives, that alliances form to advance the agenda of only some against all the rest. Critical Theorists, in sum, expect to find sin—even if most of them wouldn't use that theological term.

They look for it, however, not merely to condemn, but to diagnose society's ills and then prescribe a healthful alternative. And they maintain a guiding hope that if they can make their case clearly on the basis of sound thinking and substantial evidence about what's wrong and what could instead be right, their fellow citizens will at least eventually agree and endorse their solutions. Critical Theorists, that is, aren't merely critics and aren't merely theorists. However abstruse they can be--and some of them are abstruse indeed—their aim is constructive: literally, to build a better world.

Critical Theorists pursue, therefore, what in North American life today would generally be called progressive politics. They believe that so long as society is truly open to rational discourse—without warping or silencing by powerful interests—and particularly if once-marginal voices are given platforms so as to both augment and correct conventional opinion (which is generally the opinion of the strong), individual and communal betterment will eventually be worked out. Critical Theorists trust in the extended conversations and transactions of a liberal (= "free) culture.

Once you grasp Critical Theory, it's not hard to understand Critical Race Theory.

Critical Race Theory arose in legal studies a generation ago in the United States. It since has spread to other disciplines. To be sure, "CRT" has become a slogan used by activists on the right and the left to stand for all sorts of woke ideas and initiatives. But let's hold off on considering that form of "CRT" for the moment and learn a little more about *actual* Critical Race Theory.

Critical Race Theorists were convinced of the basic premise of Critical Theory: that the institutions of all societies can be presumed to be warped, at least a little and perhaps a lot, by the interests of those in the centre—the centre of culture, the centre of politics, the centre of power. Certain African-Americans, and later people of other ethnic backgrounds, then looked at the American legal system and found it to be exactly what Critical Theory would expect it to be: pervaded by racism, as the dominant whites tilted the legal table in their favour and against the alternatives: non-whites.

Critical Race Theory since then has gone beyond the legal sphere to look at other institutions, and it has found what it expected to find. Racism is there, too. Why? For the unsurprising reason that those with power typically use it to alter systems to their advantage.

Critical Race Theory has been caricatured as spotting racism *everywhere*, as if every single municipal parking regulation or every single speech an American president or judge ever gave was heavy with racist implication. CRT doesn't say that racism pervades everything in American life. What it says instead is that the sensible person will presume that racism is *somewhere* in the governing structures of American life, because racism is evident in the founding culture of America (slaveholding was widespread in the American colonies of the eighteenth century) and because racism has universally been convenient for slaveholders to justify their practice. Furthermore, even when slavery is officially abolished, racism continues to advantage at least some whites over non-whites. It even benefits rich whites over poor whites as it splits the working classes into mutually antagonistic racialized groups who might otherwise work together for their mutual betterment against the powers that exploit them both. (See Denzel Washington's movie *The Great Debaters* for a glimpse into that dynamic.)

CRT poses, in essence, a sharply pointed question. What, really, were the chances that the white, propertied men of the early American Republic would set up a judicial and political and economic system that didn't privilege...white, propertied men? Critical Theorists would say those chances would be, approximately, . . . zero.

Thus, the Critical Race Theorists' declaration that they have found evidence of "systemic racism" should come not as a shock but as a foregone conclusion. In the very nature of human interactions, there will likely be racism, and racism popping up all over the place—from jurisprudence to jokes.

Again, CRT isn't saying there is discernible racism in every element and every moment of American life. That would be absurd, and CRT was not, in its original form, absurd. Critical Race Theory is simply looking with realistic eyes at the basic rules and institutions of American life, set up by certain kinds of people, and finding that those rules and institutions tend to benefit those certain kinds of people. That should not surprise any of us.

Critical Race Theory is paralleled by other forms of what might broadly be called "critical theory" (without the capital letters that denote the Frankfurt School in particular). Feminist theory comes immediately to mind, of course. Patriarchy is ubiquitous, and feminist scholars and activists thus find negatively differential treatment of women virtually everywhere they look. In the very nature of human interactions, we can expect to see sexism.

Similar analyses and similar condemnations of our society have arisen in charges of homophobia, transphobia, and Islamophobia. The "Occupy" movement (so long ago, it now seems) cried out against the perpetual exploitation of the poor by the rich, and of most of us by the one per cent (and even more by the top one-tenth of one per cent). In the very nature of human interactions, there will be discrimination, if not outright, oppression. Big surprise.

So far, then, from a Christian point of view Critical Race Theory doesn't seem controversial so much as it seems incontrovertibly obvious. We Christians, of all people, should expect a battle against "unseen powers and principalities" driving earthly society. Why, then, is it in the news as something to be championed or fought?

The problem has come when scholarly work has become advocacy. So convinced are certain critical theorists (and their fans) of the correctness of their analysis and of the justice of their cause that in the name of political and ethical liberalism—of freedom, of human rights, and so on—they have become fiercely *illiberal*.

"Our opponents are manifestly and venomously wrong. Why should we tolerate a single word out of their lying mouths? Why give them a platform to advance their dangerous deceits?" Tell the truth, such zealots cry—and silence anyone who says otherwise.

Now we're into "CRT" as a political program. And it is not accidental that the furore over CRT has been a distinctly American phenomenon. Let's take a brief look at the Americanness of the CRT controversy, and then examine "anti-racism" as one of the key elements in the broader woke agenda.

As a Canadian with both personal and scholarly acquaintance of things American (I pursued graduate studies including American religious history at Wheaton College and The University of Chicago), I have been bemused by the furore lashing my southern cousins over Critical Race Theory. Why in the world is this a thing?

As I have tried to show in the preceding discussion, CRT seems like just another analytical tool, along with other critical expectations of sexism, classism, and the rest, that would be almost certainly useful in any serious examination of American culture. We often miss seeing what we aren't looking for, and CRT reminds us to look for what's likely there: white Americans, who long enslaved and to this day have a vexed relationship with Black Americans, fostering a legal system that advantages them by race. Sounds simply sensible.

So why are governors, legislatures, school boards, universities, and even churches up in arms over such a banal expectation? From a Canadian point of view, the controversy seems absurdly disproportionate.

But then, we Canadians don't think all that much of, or about, our Constitution. And Americans really, really do think that much of theirs.

We Canadians, in fact, got along nicely with a British version of our constitution from the time of original Confederation (1867) until 1982. And even now most of us can't recite a single phrase of our (new) constitutive document.

Americans, however, take oaths to "support and defend the Constitution and laws of the United States against all enemies, foreign and domestic." Not to defend *America* per se, or the United States government, or the President, or the flag, but *the Constitution and laws*, specifically.

As a Canadian living in the U.S. for a decade, I became deeply impressed—and afresh on each Fourth of July—at how Americans typically regarded the Declaration of Independence and the Constitution—and even, for some, the Federalist Papers. These documents *made* America. As such, they clearly were invested with positively sacred status.

To assume as CRT does, therefore, that the American system of jurisprudence is inherently and importantly racist is to assume that *the Constitution* is racist. And to assume that the Constitution is racist is to assume that *America* is racist.

And now we're cutting to the heart of the messianic vision of America. Here is John Winthrop's "city on a hill" (as he preached to the colonists about to found the Massachusetts Bay colony in 1630), the beacon of light to old Europe, the nation whose Manifest Destiny it has been to rule North America and extend liberty, democracy, and free enterprise to the world.

To assume systemic racism in American jurisprudence is to assume that America is, in fact, not a, or even the, Christian Nation but a Bad Nation.

So now we're in the realm, not of different scholarly interpretations of the history of the American legal system, but of fidelity versus treachery, loyalty versus sedition.

Now the outrage—for that is what so much of this reaction surely is—makes sense.

The informed Canadian might shake her head at this turmoil. Is it really news that America has a race problem—a deep and broad race problem—going back at least to 1776 (or 1619)? It surely isn't. But what goes far deeper than the sting of prodded conscience for Americans outraged by CRT is the wound of assailing the very web that holds America together as an idea. CRT threatens the structure that bound the original thirteen colonies and that binds the disparate fifty States into something United to this day. Attacking the Constitution makes you a domestic enemy. And Americans know what to do with enemies.

And yet. And yet. Even a Canadian with only a nodding acquaintance with things American knows that in that very Constitution seems confirmation of the entire CRT agenda.

Article one, section two of the Constitution of the United States used to declare that any person who was not free would be counted as three-fifths of a free individual for the purposes of determining congressional representation. This is a clause transparently uninterested in the welfare of those unfree (nonwhite) persons but designed instead to determine how many (white) men would be named to the federal government.

Sure, that notorious clause has been replaced by the thirteenth and fourteenth amendments. But when even your sacred Constitution requires that much remediation, what else might need spotting and fixing?

Indeed, when CRT can make its case just that immediately, the friendly outsider worries that these disputes about CRT will not soon be reduced to mere disputes about . . . CRT. 'Way too much is at stake, since the very question of national loyalty has been put front and center.

Anti-racism now appears on the cultural scene to warn us that discovering racism and working against it is not just for CRT proponents, not just for activists or those victimized by racism, but for every conscientious person. If you aren't actively resisting racism, you are implicitly condoning it. And that provocation deserves a longer look.

Chapter Six

Anti-Racism

Who can possibly be against such basic human values as diversity, equity, and inclusion (DEI)? Who would dare to argue against the commonsense realism of Critical Race Theory (CRT)?

Lots of people, apparently—from talk-show hosts ranting against wokeism to politicians seeking to expose and root out any trace of CRT and DEI from every school, business, and government agency.

Some such might resist DEI initiatives out of lingering prejudices and hatreds. Some people evidently loathe anyone visibly different from themselves. Some people despise people of the other sex, or of a different sexuality, or of a novel gender identity.

Many other people see CRT as an intellectual toxin poisoning the minds especially of impressionable youth against the inherent goodness of their nation, its laws, and its mission. They crusade against CRT because CRT threatens to tear apart the social fabric in an unrelenting storm of insatiable suspicion.

Not everyone unhappy about DEI or CRT is foaming at the mouth, however. Others of us have quietly become wary of such campaigns and are not yet convinced we should climb aboard this bandwagon. In fact, some of us fear that what is being offered in our schools and workplaces is not the apparently benign and humble recognition of prejudice such that we can cooperate together better than before. What we may be getting instead is a malignant and arrogant insistence on perpetual race warfare, implacably opposed conceptions of sex and gender, and constant class struggle. What actually threatens our common life is a Manichean battle of good against evil, angels against demons, with no possible resolution, therefore, except the complete victory of one side over another.

The dark irony, then, is that diversity, equity, and inclusion, in some cases, arrives only on the strict terms of the woke. Such multiculturalism refuses to make room for conservative ideologies, and particularly conservative religions, Christianity above all.

A particular phrase has been added to this conversation—and these campaigns—that indeed divides the world into two kinds of people. We need to get it in focus before we proceed to discuss the Big Picture and how to respond to it.

"Anti-racism" as a general term stands for just what you think it stands for: convictions and actions that identify, denounce, and combat racism. And what is racism? Negative prejudice about and negative treatment of people based on supposed racial inferiority.

Alas, certain writers and speakers have been trading on the genuine scholarship of Critical Race Theory and the moral popularity of what we might call *generic* anti-racism to assert something quite particular: that white Americans are necessarily racist just by being white Americans. (Similar charges have been made about white Canadians, white Britons, and others, but the main arena so far has been the United States.)

The most sensible version of this anti-racist argument—so far as I understand it—goes like this. The basic institutions of American society are fundamentally racist—shaped by white people to advantage themselves and their descendants against all others. All white people therefore benefit from those institutions merely by being white. Any white person who does not therefore commit himself or herself to an active program of anti-racism—in all of one's life, public and private—is implicitly colluding with this racist regime.

The logic seems to be that of the moral binary and political polarization. The whole system is corrupt, so the only ethical response is conscious and constant resistance. Anything less than that is de facto racism, refusing to challenge an unjust system and therefore collaborating with it—however unwittingly. What goes for individuals, of course, goes for companies, and schools, and healthcare systems, and everything and everybody. So now alongside the positive ideals of diversity, equity, and inclusion every citizen, including every corporate citizen, must also embrace anti-racism.

The most plausible way to see why this isn't just doubletalk is to understand that, in this view of things, justice will not be achieved merely by adding diversity and inclusivity to the workplace, or classroom, or congregation, or neighbourhood. The company, the university, the church, and the city are inherently corrupt with racism. So what's bad needs to be identified, denounced, and dealt with even as what's good needs to be increased.

Well, who can be against anti-racism (to invoke a triple negative)—besides racists, of course? Who can be against anti-sexism initiatives, or anti-homophobia policies? Why are American legislators up in arms against CRT? Why doesn't everyone welcome DEI?

Again, from a Christian point of view, some of the resistance to anti-racism, CRT, and DEI surely stems from sin. Many of us do benefit from racism, sexism, and other forms of discrimination. We assure ourselves that *we* never use bad words, *we* like our diverse colleagues, and even some of our best friends are . . ., etc.

But the social system in the United States—sometimes identified with awful oversimplification as just "America"—has helped white Americans get where they are. Threats to that system mean threats to *me*, if I'm white—and to my great country. So now anti-racism is no longer just about me and my shortcoming as insufficiently woke, but about my nation and my heritage. And that might provoke more than a little defensiveness.

We may not even acknowledge consciously that we don't want things to change. But *we don't want things to change*—which is evident in our *not* changing things, and in our resenting those who try to do so. So there's that. Fair point.

Still, you don't have to be a white American to fret about what in some situations nowadays looks like a left-wing political and social campaign matched with a whole industry of well-paid and imperious reformers. Here they come: into our offices and conference rooms, and into our children's classes, with mandatory seminars rife with accusations that all the white people in the room are racist (unless they can present sufficient antiracist credentials—receipts, as it were) and assurances that everyone else is a victim entitled to feelings of resentment and claims for reparations.

Indeed, a more insidious version of CRT says that people racialized as white are incapable of sincere anti-racism. (I say "racialized" because there is no such thing as "race" beyond social constructions. All there is to "race" is whatever convenient conventions of this or that culture or subculture that serve to put some people in a nicely graded hierarchy according to stereotypes of appearance—literally, discrimination that is "skin deep.") *Interest convergence* is the term here that accuses white people of being willing to help those who are racialized differently only insofar as it is in white people's interest to do so. Such a view damns white people as irredeemably racist while people of colour enjoy an automatic moral superiority.

Are we therefore now mired in racism? How do we move forward? It's not as if there is no actual problem of racism in the United States—or Canada, or Australia, or the U.K. There is. It's not as if we live in a promised land of diversity, equity, and inclusion. We don't. Yet the holy war of some activists rightly alarms many people, especially conservative-minded Christians, who should nonetheless agree with the basic concerns of DEI and CRT.

What should progress look like now? For some people, it seems, the place to start is in changing other people's language. In making sure other people use proper terminology. Could that make the world a much better place? You guessed it: it's time to consider political correctness.

Chapter Seven

Political Correctness

Political correctness is hardly news. Three decades ago, Henry Beard and Christopher Cerf produced *The Official Politically Correct Dictionary and Handbook* (Villard, 1992) to guide us satirically through the maze of appropriate discourse.

One might previously have said, "See that bald, white man over there sitting with his pet dog and reading a newspaper?" Now, however, one would say, "See that hair-disadvantaged, melanin-impoverished human animal over there sitting with his protector and reading a processed tree carcass?"

One might overhear someone suggest, "You won't get warts if you kiss a toad; that's just an old wives' tale," but one ought to have heard, "You won't get warts if you kiss a nonhuman amphibian animal; that's just a longer-lived unpaid sex worker's tale."

And in particularly scrupulous circles, one might have avoided the word "woman" in favour of "wofem," "womban," "womon," "womyn," "woperson," or "person of gender"—anything to avoid linking one sex to the other.

What made the Beard and Cerf collection provocative a generation ago was that most of their examples came from actual, documented cases. And what used to be an issue afflicting progressive university campuses has become a culture-wide debate.

Very simply, "political correctness" (PC) denotes a constraint upon certain ideas and expressions in our society, and especially in particular institutional sectors in our society such as government, law, and education. This constraint is exercised on behalf of oppressed or marginalized groups, whether women, ethnic minorities, the disabled, and so on. Ideas, policies, and activities that are seen to promote the welfare of such groups are affirmed in the current climate; those that do not are "politically *in*correct" and are met with animosity and even remedial coercion.

Let's focus here upon politically correct speech, since that is the zone in which most of us will feel the pressure to change. And there is much to dislike in this zone.

First, of course, is the very question of freedom of speech. Our culture is built on the liberal democratic principle that the truth—and, along with it, the good and the beautiful—is most likely to emerge and to flourish amid the welter of competing alternatives in a wide-open forum unpoliced by anyone or any ideology. Aside from certain cases in which speech must be regulated for everyone's benefit—in regard to contracts, for instance, or defamation, or public safety (so one can't falsely call out "Fire!"in a crowded theatre, a rule that emerged when fires in early cinemas were not uncommon)—we have generally agreed on the basic principle of free speech. PC speech codes seem directly inimical to this principle, enshrining instead just one set of values above all others.

Second, PC stipulations can seem damaging, chilling, and misleading. They imply that people of manifest goodwill and intelligence are wicked and stupid for not keeping up with and abiding by the latest terminology. They keep us from hearing important things from people cowed by fear of putting a linguistic foot wrong. And they can confuse us (as in the examples above) as they avoid conventional English for language writhing to avoid offense, avoiding actual communication in the process.

Writing in *The Atlantic*, George Packer warns,

> The whole tendency of equity language is to blur the contours of hard, often unpleasant facts. This aversion to reality is its main appeal. Once you acquire the vocabulary, it's actually easier to say *people with limited financial resources* than *the poor*. The first rolls off your tongue without interruption, leaves no aftertaste, arouses no emotion. The second is rudely blunt and bitter, and it might make someone angry or sad. Imprecise language is less likely to offend.

Imprecise language is also less likely to *motivate*: to urge us to do something to help *poor* people, not merely—and the implied "merely" is precisely the problem—those *with limited financial resources.*

Third, PC lexica are vulnerable to scorn, with the baleful implication that the generally laudable concerns and goals of most political correctness come in for contempt as well. Genuinely traumatized people who deserve thoughtful consideration in the form of a reasonable accommodation—perhaps simply a courteous "content (or trigger) warning"—get lumped in with the excessively sensitive as "snowflakes."

And it is tempting to see the whole PC agenda merely as a self-aggrandizing diversion of intellectuals who have given up trying to make any substantial social change on behalf of justice to settle instead for playing with language.

And so we return to the wise words Kong-zi (Confucius) who urged us to begin all serious thought with "the rectification of names"—or, more simply, naming things properly. And in terms of justice-seeking, Christians share many concerns with our progressive neighbours of various stripes such that we should want to govern our language accordingly.

After all, many of the causes PC embraces are manifestly good causes from a Christian point of view. Not every one of them are good, of course, and Christians must exercise compassionate but also keen discernment of godly norms regarding each case.

Yet who can deny the long history of female subjugation to men? Who can dispute the history of prejudice against ethnic minorities? Who can dismiss the history of selfish thoughtlessness about the disabled, the poor, the widow, the orphan? Who can seriously maintain that all of these persons and groups are equally and fairly treated today?

Christians ought to champion the welfare of all members of our society as equally valuable to our loving God (as many Christians have championed such causes in the past). And whatever can help in this righteous cause surely deserves Christian support.

More particularly, it can be salutary indeed to be urged to "watch our language" regarding those other than ourselves and our kind. When I attended The University of Chicago fresh out of the evangelical Wheaton College Graduate School in the early 1980s, I quickly intuited that I had better keep my guard up and my head down. I had to drop some of my favourite jokes. I had to switch to gender-inclusive language, never again assuming that my hearers would happily understand (let alone welcome) "he" and "man" as generic. Before long, I was second-guessing my words every time I raised a question in class, every time I conversed over lunch with other students, every time I wrote a paper. And such self-consciousness was thoroughly and completely worthwhile.

I learned not to offend people I didn't mean to offend. I learned to stretch my own concepts out of a privileged, white, male, heterosexual, North American mindset to include lots of other people too—to at least begin to take account of other points of view more naturally, more reflexively, than ever before. And I developed a light-footedness in addressing pluralized groups, a nimbleness in switching terms so as to include as many as possible. By doing so, I could help focus their minds on the main point I was making, rather than distracting and alienating them by some unconscious social-linguistic faux pas.

As Christians, we ought to use considerate speech. We ought to, "so far as it depends on [us], live peaceably with all" (Rom. 12:18 NRSV). Especially in the cause of mission, we must be sensitive to language—every bit as much as foreign missionaries must be sensitive to language in their cross-cultural contexts. How do we hope to win the attention and appreciation of others if we offend them on secondary issues? (This is why, among other reasons, Christians ought to use Bible translations in public worship that consistently use inclusive language for human beings.)

Beyond our concern for others' sensibilities, however, it is good for us to become more aware of "different others," to take other points of view into account more readily. Our own thinking about the world, and acting in the world, will broaden and deepen as we adopt other perspectives. Such habits of sensitivity are necessary to promote the healthy functioning of a continually pluralizing society. And Christians of all people ought to be in the vanguard of promoting such corporate wellbeing.

George Parker's observation, in fact, works the other way as well. It is commonplace among scholars of so-called ethnic cleansing that those targeted for oppression are routinely referred to in sub-human terms: "cockroach," "rat," and the like. Just as referring to a poor person as "income-challenged" doesn't prompt much compassion, referring to someone as *vermin* doesn't prompt the respect he or she deserves but quite the opposite. We act as we think, and if we think there's no big ethical issue here, we won't act as if there is a big ethical issue here.

Long before we get to the enormities of genocide, moreover, there is the perpetration of subordination in the gentle insults of diminutive language: calling any woman in a serving role "honey" or "babe," or a Black man "boy." (Sidney Pollack's groundbreaking comedy *Tootsie* skewers sexist language the way just about any movie portraying white-Black relations in the southern U.S.A. before, say, 1980 skewers the casual racism of that region.) Feminist scholars and activists have understandably encouraged women to object to such demeaning forms of address. Mountains of systemic discrimination can indeed be made out of molehills of microaggression. There is a real problem here, therefore, and perhaps social pressure on our speech, if not outright regulation, can help with it.

Furthermore, as Christians rooted in the Bible we have a heritage of obeying implicit and explicit regulations that encourage righteousness. So the mere idea of regulations should not be rejected at first blush.

External regulations cannot in themselves change the heart, of course. But they can help to create a new set of social arrangements in which new, better attitudes are more likely to emerge. And even if they don't emerge, the regulations can curtail injury done by one group to another, can blunt and soften vocabularies that heretofore have cut people cruelly. Regulations on speech, as well as on other actions, can restrain evil among people even if they cannot root out or transform the evil within them. Those who have historically been marginalized by language must find it safe to engage fully with the rest of us, and they cannot if they feel insulted by common references to them.

Still, however, I remain deeply disquieted by the ever-changing and ever-expanding domain of "acceptable" speech, and even more by the doctrinaire and authoritarian regimes that insist on it and enforce it. Increasing appreciation for "the other" is good. Paralysis from self-censorship is bad. And the sanctimonious silencing of anyone innocently ignorant of the latest code update narrows the conversation to a mere rally of the agreed.

To be woke in this extreme sense, therefore, is to be arrogantly judgmental—and *that* can't be right. So how should a Christian think better about all that woke means today?

Part Two

Chapter Eight

Christians and Liberal Politics

I was raised to believe that true Christians are to stand against all things *liberal*. Lots of other people in North America and beyond have been similarly trained. In fact, however, most of what we call "liberal" in our culture has roots in Christianity.

Let's start on some broadly common ground—and it will surprise some readers once more to realize how common it is. When it comes to *liberalism*, let's remind ourselves that almost all readers of this booklet are in fact *political* liberals of one hue or another. We all value universal human rights, government only by popular consent, votes for all competent adults, respect for private property and the rule of law, and so on. That's historically what political liberalism meant—over against, say, the divine right of kings or the dictatorship of a fascist leader or a communist party.

Moreover, while many of the great thinkers of *cultural* or *ethical* liberalism have eschewed anything like orthodox Christianity (such as John Stuart Mill in the nineteenth century or John Rawls in the twentieth), many others have rooted themselves in the Christian tradition, or at least found it to provide us with values without which liberalism cannot function (from the great English philosopher John Locke to Germany's Critical Theorist Jürgen Habermas). So there is no inherent problem for the serious Christian when it comes to political liberalism in this broad sense of the term.

It should be noted that *theological* liberalism is a different thing altogether. This tradition, usually traced to F. D. E. Schleiermacher at the turn of the nineteenth century, differs from orthodox theology in both method and substance. Liberal theology feels itself to be free (Latin *liber*) to harvest what it finds helpful in the Christian heritage—whether Scripture or tradition—to illuminate and supplement the best of contemporary thought. If this Biblical book or revered author or creed of the Church helps us think better about justice, for instance, then we gladly draw from it. But if any book or author or creed speaks in what we now find to be objectionable ways, we are free to leave it in the past. It has no binding authority over our theological freedom.

This methodological liberty resulted in characteristic redefinitions of basic Christian doctrines. Schleiermacher famously (or notoriously) found the doctrine of the Trinity to be not so much a mystery to be revered as a confusion to be jettisoned. Jesus was not the incarnation of a supposed Second Person of a triune God but was instead a human being so full of God-consciousness, so suffused with godliness, that to meet him was *as if* one were encountering God in the Redeemer (Schleiermacher's favourite term for Christ). Jesus was thus the first Christian, so to speak, and Christianity was then defined in one or another combination of mysticism and moralism, of piety and practice. Gone was the traditional (and, to certain modern sensibilities, repellent) scheme of divine ferocity against sin being appeased by the propitiatory sacrifice of the crucified Lamb of God. Here instead was a bright, hopeful religion of spiritual connection with the Divine (however one freely defines it) prompting the pursuit of righteousness by well-motivated people in a troubled world. As the Yale theologian H. Richard Niebuhr summed it up, albeit somewhat acidly, "A God without wrath brought men without sin to a kingdom without judgment through the ministrations of a Christ without a Cross" (*The Kingdom of God in America*, 1937).

Liberalism in this theological sense is *not* what we're talking about here, and many Christians have to learn to distinguish *religious* liberalism from *cultural* or *political* liberalism. There is no inherent connection between them, just as there is no inherent connection between conservative Christianity and conservative politics per se (especially since what counts as "conservative politics" has ranged from defending a monarchy to defending the smallest possible government). Theologically liberal Christians might be fierce libertarians on the American political right—or, for that matter, fierce monarchists on the British political right, and many liberal Christians supported National Socialism in Germany (as did, of course, other Christians across the spectrum). Orthodox Christians, for their part, have been supporters of left-of-centre political parties throughout the Anglosphere and across Europe for two centuries now. Such believers have campaigned on the front lines of many progressive causes, from the abolition of slavery to the eradication of child labour to the franchise being extended to women and the poor.

As for *socialism*, much of European politics since the end of the Second World War has been affected by groups identified with *democratic socialism* and also, confusingly enough, *social democracy*. Democratic socialists tend toward a socialist, rather than a capitalist, economy, while social democrats seek to temper capitalism with a compassionate and just welfare state. Complicating the picture still further, German politics in particular has been dominated by *Christian democracy*, a version of politics strongly influenced by Catholic social thought and the neo-Calvinism of Dutch prime minister Abraham Kuyper. Hard to pinpoint on a simple political spectrum, it has typically been understood as centre-left in economics while being centre-right on many social issues. The Christian Democratic Union has so prevailed in Germany that it is often referred to as the "natural governing party" of that country.

Canadian politics also has been influenced deeply by socialist concerns, whether explicitly—as in the New Democratic Party, whose most prominent and effective leader was the Baptist preacher Tommy Douglas—or piecemeal by the Liberals and even Conservatives at times. Indeed, policies that used to be identified with the left in Canada, and still are in the United States and elsewhere, have become so mainstream in Canada, the United Kingdom, the Nordics, and beyond that they nowadays are simply taken for granted: (un)employment insurance, universal single-payer (so-called "free") health insurance, social security, and more. Down Under, socialism has emerged along a spectrum from Labour parties to communist organizations in both Australia and New Zealand. And in all of these countries, a variety of socialist concerns have emerged in Green parties foregrounding environmental concerns at a time when people across the political spectrum express worry about global climate change.

Only in the United States, therefore, are socialists generally homeless in the major political parties. The campaigns of Sen. Bernie Sanders to become the Democratic nominee for president and the more radical utterances of the so-called "Squad" in the U.S. Congress have been the only mainstream socialist options in America of late.

May I say therefore to my American cousins that *there is nothing inherently anti-Christian about socialism*, let alone left-leaning politics more generally. Many socialists, to be sure, have resented the Church's alignment with established power and thus have sounded anti-Christian. But criticism of a particular church in a particular society at a particular time can hardly be seen as evidence of antipathy toward the true religion of Jesus. Martin Luther, Blaise Pascal, John Wesley, Søren Kierkegaard, and Martin Luther King—just to pick easily recognizable representatives from each of the last five centuries—quite openly criticized the dominant churches of their day, and most orthodox Christians now would revere them as champions of authentic faith. Socialism in any given situation might be a questionable option—I'm not inclined to it myself—but it isn't inherently a wicked option.

We all agree that in some situations government control is the least bad option. Socialists simply extend that jurisdiction farther than some of the rest of us would. Thus the political debate continues—among socialists, as well as among the rest of us.

Communism, to be sure, has generally been anti-Christian. (The occasional Christian experiment in collectivism is the exception to the rule.) Marx and Engels, and most communists ever since, have viewed Christianity as among the leading social problems that communism was meant to solve. The Christian religion, as they have seen it, served only the interests of the powerful. Christianity was in truth a deceptively attractive ideology that legitimized the perpetual control of capital by the rich while offering false consolation of a happy world to come—and a sense that obeying God in the present one meant remaining quiescent and cooperative—to their victims. The communists weren't entirely wrong in their critique, of course, both in their place and time and indeed in ours. Elites in Christian societies have indeed cynically called upon Christian values to justify their position and keep everyone else in their places. But the solution offered by communism normally includes the destruction of Christianity root and branch, not a return to its Christ-centered ideals. Since I daresay communism is therefore not a live option for the readers of this book—socialists themselves oppose any sort of Marxist-Leninist or Maoist totalitarianism—we'll leave it at that.

To reiterate this chapter's crucial point, therefore: there is no inherent connection between liberal politics and liberal Christianity—whether in the broad sense of the liberal political tradition or in the more recent sense of left-of-centre political philosophies and parties. Christ-honouring, churchgoing, Bible-believing Christians in centuries past and in our own day not only have taken for granted the general principles of the general liberal political tradition, but have adopted various forms of progressive politics to advance Biblical justice, compassion, and beauty for everyone, using the means of democratic government and the economic and social possibilities of a free society. (Again, please be clear that I do not defend outright *communism* at all!) Whether in small Christian communities of solidarity with the poor evident among evangelicals in Latin America, in the fervent house churches of China, in the "new monasticism" among evangelicals in the United States, or in left-of-centre political parties in Britain, Canada, Australia, New Zealand, the Nordics, Germany, and Czechia, a wide range of political and social and cultural options are open for legitimate, if also critical, evangelical consideration.

Chapter Nine

Christians and Critical Race Theory

What, then, about all the (mostly, but not entirely) American fuss regarding Critical Race Theory? Is it a clever form of reverse racism against white people? Is it anti-American? And even if it is, how is it a threat to Christians, as so many Christians seem to be saying it is?

Let's start briefly with Critical Theory. As we have seen, its basic premise can hardly be disputed from a Christian vantage point. Power does tend to corrupt, as (the Christian) Lord Acton observed. Moreover, those Protestants who affirm the doctrine of total depravity—the idea that all of our selves, not just certain parts of our selves, is deeply affected by sin—shouldn't have trouble accepting a social version of this idea. Such Christians would simply *assume* that every institution harbours at least *some* corruption of motives and modes. Every sector of life is warped by the powerful in their own interest.

To be sure, just as the doctrine of total depravity doesn't mean that we are each as wicked as we could be (as if we were *totally depraved*), Critical Theory doesn't expect that everything everywhere is hopelessly rotten. If CT did say that, it wouldn't prompt the energetic varieties of political reform that it manifestly has fostered. Why bother trying to reform something that is hopelessly corrupt? Critical Theorists try to change things for the better because they believe that things can be changed for the better.

Most Christians, furthermore, will agree with the Critical Theorists that the extended project of democratic negotiation is the best (which is to say, as Churchill did, the least bad) of the available forms of government. We Christians should be more dubious than at least some of the Critical Theorists about how good the outcomes will be, since we have a robust doctrine of sin. Christians want Jesus to return not least because we know that every government between now and then will deeply disappoint, even as some are markedly better than others. But, yes, we are committed to the democratic project, albeit with our eyes steadfastly open to whatever Critical Theory can expose to our gaze.

How about Critical Race Theory, then?

Christians not only can be sympathetic to it, but basically *agree* with it, as we should with any related critical theory. Why? Because Christians likewise presume that institutions are everywhere and always bent to fit the agenda of the powerful. To quote the Beloved Disciple, "the whole world lies under the power of the evil one" (I John 5:19).

If white Christian men run the show, you can bet—from a Christian point of view—that nonwhite, non-Christian non-men will be discriminated against in some fashion. And, yes, we likely need to acknowledge here that men and women of colour espousing other ideologies in other situations also have been capable of great institutional injustice and violence. That's part of our doctrine regarding fallen human nature. We sinners *all* tend to use our power to our own advantage, rather than follow the Biblical principle of using our power to advantage others. No surprises there.

Let's be clear that those white Christian men might not consciously mean to discriminate. Some may even take up the cause of justice on behalf of others. But as the history of actual campaigns for emancipation and equality shows, even on the side of justice, the powerful tend to treat the less powerful differently—and worse. Patriarchy, for instance, suffused much of the abolitionist movement. Racism shows up in the history of feminism. Even the famous Clapham Sect led by William Wilberforce generally left intact, because uncriticized, both major social structures and prevailing social attitudes that continued to harm Britain's poor.

Christians, like any other thoughtful people, will reserve the right and responsibility, of course, to disagree with this or that version of Critical Race Theory—or feminism, or any other ideology—and especially if it is itself tending toward hatred. Christians should insist that everyone be *loved*, not hated—including our enemies. Christians will insist that, so far as we can tell (since we cannot X-ray hearts), everyone at least potentially can be redeemed by God. And Christians will insist that utopia will come only with the reign of the returned Lord Jesus. So we will neither expect to witness all wrongs being righted, nor be discouraged when our campaigns fail to achieve all their goals. Nonetheless, Christians should stand with all who contend for justice and compassion, even as we will differ with some of our neighbours (and even among ourselves) as to strategy and tactics in the quest to make peace, to make shalom. There is no obviously One Correct Road to Happy Valley available to us. (Maranatha.)

In the next chapter, we will guard against those who would use DEI, CRT, and anti-racism to perpetuate, ironically enough, division, systemic oppression, and racism. Here, however, we will aver a realistic hope, a sensible prudence toward making shalom in public and in private.

So far, then, Critical Race Theory doesn't seem controversial so much as it seems, especially from a Christian point of view, obvious. Thoughtful Christians can and should draw upon CRT when critically assessing our society's legal, economic, political, and cultural structures. Why would we *not* look carefully for racism—or sexism, or classism, and the like?

To be sure, reducing the study of anything—laws, literature, biography, religion—merely to these questions of possible discrimination can become an exercise in tedious bitterness. I suffered through more than one Ph.D. historical seminar in which certain students relentlessly criticized books from previous decades or even centuries for failing to manifest up-to-the-minute social enlightenment. More and more scholars today rightly lament the study of literature being reduced instead to politics, with no regard for style, craft, or insight into humanity, let alone delight in reading fine work. Against such narrowmindedness we need to push back. What good *is* there to be found and enjoyed in these important works?

Yes, we can and should note any deficiencies. Recognition of such helps us get the authors and writings into better focus. At the same time, perhaps those marginalized or racialized persons who would be re-traumatized by reading such historical works shouldn't merely be forced to read them. That is the challenge of creating equitable study plans. But sensible people must guard against any reductionism in the academy, however commendably motivated by a quest for justice.

CRT, therefore, must be used properly as a tool and not raised grotesquely to an all-encompassing outlook. If it is thus used, therefore, why is it in the news as something to be championed or fought? The problem has come when scholarly work has become *advocacy*, and advocacy has become *censorship* and *coercion*. So convinced are certain critical theorists (and their fans) of the correctness of their analysis and of the justice of their cause that in the name of political and ethical liberalism—of freedom, of human rights, and so on—they have become fiercely illiberal.

Their judgmental attitude does have a certain logic. Why give any oxygen to manifestly repellent ideas? Isn't allowing them even a moment's attention a kind of legitimation?

Now we're into "CRT" and "DEI" as a political program alongside "anti-racism," and now things get dangerous.

Chapter Ten

Christians and the Politics of Diversity

Once more we must ask, who can possibly be against diversity, equity, and inclusion (DEI)?

Christians will want to support such initiatives completely—when doing so is (1) a matter of justice, treating people properly who weren't treated properly before, and (2) a policy that will improve the situation. But let's park on this second point a moment.

Particularly when it comes to hiring practices, some people understandably resist DEI initiatives for fear that underqualified people will be preferred. Pressing "diversity" too far could mean that the best person for the job won't get it. That is a genuine danger. But it's worth considering that hiring is normally about joining a team, not just getting a job. And in many instances increasing diversity improves the team. A good football team cannot be composed entirely of quarterbacks, no matter how talented.

Some kinds of diversity won't make such a difference, of course. But being female, or Black, or Korean often can help a team see things, and imagine things, and say things, and do things it wouldn't do, or do as well, without such diversity. So when diversity matters, it matters. DEI policies require us to think about larger issues than just individuals and individual situations.

The same goes for CRT and the anti-racism agenda, and even for sensible forms of speech codes. Christians ought to be on the alert for sin in societal structures just the way we expect sin in individuals. (Indeed, groups often function worse—think of mob "justice"—than each of their constituent individuals would behave on his or her own. Reinhold Niebuhr once ruefully remarked that he ought to have retitled his famous book *Immoral Man and Even More Immoral Society*.)

Why, then, the huge and continuing uproar? Why are so many people frightened and furious about anything woke?

Once again we must ruefully acknowledge that some of those people are patently racists, sexists, homophobes, or the like. They certainly aren't all like that, to be sure. I acknowledge that conscientious people, even Christians, could vote for Donald Trump in a presidential election as the better of the two available alternatives. I have friends and family members who did so, and I don't question their integrity. They themselves would agree, however, that the Trump era in America, along with the rise of similar alt-right movements in Europe, the U.K., Canada, and Australasia, has given social permission for many more awful people to make much more awful noise in public. Much of the reaction against anything woke manifestly comes from people fiercely protecting their prejudices and privileges.

Others of us, however, appreciate the injustice yet have specific and grave misgivings about particular programs flying under the banners of DEI, CRT, anti-racism, and political correctness. And these folk are not just on the political right. Lots of progressives are themselves appalled at consciousness-raising DEI sessions that resemble "struggle sessions" of Maoist bullies. Lots of progressives are themselves appalled at CRT advocates ignoring or even mocking the inspiring ideals of the Declaration of Independence and the American Constitution. Lots of progressives are themselves appalled at universities, public libraries, and other bastions of free speech de-platforming speakers whose views are judged to be harmful to the public good simply because the elites in charge disagree with them (or they are much more concerned about their jobs and funding), just as those progressives also fret about speech codes serving to obscure and obstruct, rather than clarify and improve, free speech about difficult and important issues.

Christians, and other sensible people, therefore, will support a woke agenda—but with three crucial qualifications.

First, when it comes to diversity, equity, inclusion, and anti-racism concerns (which I will now include for simplicity's sake as "DEI"), including people is good—except when it isn't. DEI cannot be extended to people who will disrupt our common mission and compromise the common good. Including people who will then turn on others in denunciation and excommunication, who will insist that everyone not just tolerate them but fully affirm them, destroys the very inclusivity at which DEI aims. Those who will cynically exploit the liberal welcome to then, once safely inside the circle, savage their enemies must themselves be excluded as simply making impossible any meaningful common life.

The point must be crystalline here. Such people are not to be excluded because they are advocates for this or that position some of us might find uncomfortable or even objectionable: trans rights, or gender fluidity, or reparations for racial injustice, or equal representation of women and men. They must be excluded because they advocate illiberal intolerance. They vandalize the very society that embraces them. They promote a dictatorship of the aggrieved.

Adoption of DEI policies therefore must not be construed to mean full-throated ethical endorsement of *all* diversity. The encouragement of

DEI must not be imposed as the affirmation of just anyone and anything. No society can tolerate agents working directly against it. Such people must be silenced and sidelined.

Likewise, if anyone, including any Christian, produces evidence to suggest that the accommodation of this difference and that person will militate against the common purpose and project, then he or she must be welcome to speak up and have the group at least consider that concern. The "oppressed group *du jour*" simply cannot have everything their way. And those who blow the whistle on such attempts at domination should be congratulated, not chided. Such a realistic policy requires, of course, that we sort out what is genuine harm from merely *potential* danger. We must go on to distinguish actual *danger* from mere *discomfort* that simply must be endured as we tolerate people with views we find upsetting. Such discernment, furthermore, will require that we exercise wise democratic policies, including the appropriate protection of minority rights in tandem with the fundamental commitment to the institutional mission of the company, school, or agency.

Such discernment, finally, will also require common sense. Not every microaggression is a form of oppression, and we must be careful not to dilute the meaning of (genuine) oppression. Sometimes mistakes, yes, even small ones, do deserve attention. Little things can mean a lot. But a sense of proportion must be maintained. Not every awkward situation is a crucial battle in the cosmic struggle of Good vs. Evil.

Second, we must beware of the cult of affirmation. I recall a friend of mine taking over as president of a leading Canadian university. When I visited him in his new office, I asked him about his aspirations for our *alma mater*, as we had been classmates there as undergraduates. He replied that he hoped to institute a culture of *affirmation*, not merely of *toleration*.

"Oh," I said, "I hope not."

"What do you mean?" he said, clearly bewildered. "Affirmation is so much more positive! Toleration is a mere grudging thing."

I said that I understood the difference. But then I told him a parable of sorts. I said that when our three boys were at the age to start dating girls, their mother and I offered them a choice of two policies as to which girls would be allowed in our house: a policy of affirmation or a policy of tolerance.

Our intelligent sons quickly chose tolerance over affirmation. Why? *More girls*. If only the girls their parents would *affirm* would be allowed in, they would have fewer female guests. Tolerance turned out to be the more expansive position, and affirmation the more restrictive.

This sense that *affirmation* is "nicer" than *tolerance* makes perfect sense. *Of course* is it more pleasant to be surrounded by people one can affirm: pleasant for them, pleasant for you. But the implication is obvious that there will be many fewer people in your company as you restrict such company to the quality of the *affirmable*. This creeping paradox of *affirmation as narrow hegemony* needs to be seen for what it is: a serious compromise of historic liberal freedoms, of any robust sense of diversity, equality, and inclusion, and instead the imposition of a new orthodoxy.

Toleration of non-essential differences not everyone likes is the mark of a properly adult person and a properly realistic society. Diversity can be actively pursued, furthermore, as both just and helpful, for the reasons we have outlined. Insistence, however, that everyone in an organization or in society at large must publicly and even privately affirm whatever the leaders have embraced as their peculiar moral vision must be named as what it is: authoritarian, anti-democratic, and unacceptable.

Freedom of conscience, including freedom of speech, freedom of religion, freedom of assembly, and so on must be defended except in instances that truly interfere with the healthy life of the institution. They must be defended especially when leaders face dissent, and even when someone's feelings happen to get hurt—even if that someone is the president.

Indeed, each of us must be careful not to insist in the name of affirmation, let alone in the name of justice, that everyone in a particular group—a company or a school or a church—affirm everything about me that I want affirmed. Here is where diversity, equity, and inclusion are in tension with each other, and we must soberly acknowledge that tension. If we are going to promote DEI, and in general I think we should, then it simply follows that we will have to abide the presence of people who aren't like us and who maybe don't like us—or, at least, something about us: our view of X or our preference for Y. It is contradictory, truly hypocritical, to ask to be included in the name of DEI and then refuse to extend the same inclusion to others who are diverse in ways we don't affirm, and who in turn don't affirm everything about *us*. We must content ourselves with *tolerating* and *being tolerated* in turn. Too bad if not everyone likes everything about everybody. Welcome to the real world—and the real requirements of real diversity, equity, and inclusion.

We need to recover and defend the liberal (recall *liber* = "free) commitment to freedom: freedom to be different, to think differently, to say different things, to act in different ways. Too many people nowadays—on both the left and the right—are so convinced of the correctness and virtue of their cause that they would happily impose their values on everyone else. Christians in particular need to speak up for the freedom of even our enemies to act like human beings and to be treated with the dignity of God-given freedom, however loathsome we might find their views. As the American political scientist Glenn Tinder has warned, we Christians especially must watch out that we don't grant people less liberty than God does.

Third, the woke term "intersectionality" reminds us to beware misleading binaries. Not everything comes down to black versus white—or First Nations versus settlers, or women versus men, or poor versus rich: a clearly identifiable "us versus them." We are each more than one thing, and social situations are often complex. Some people suffer multiple layers of prejudice. Alliances can and should form on multiple levels. And social ills sometimes require multiple levels of remediation—not just a relatively easy fixing of what might seem to be the most obvious issue.

Still, from a Christian point of view, DEI seems like a good idea, not least because its opposite is *sameness*, *unfairness*, and *exclusion* of everyone not just like us—hardly Christian values. So here are four red flags to watch for, signs that have helped me see what's going on when some of the CRT activists speak up and the mandatory anti-racism seminars start up.

Blame instead of analysis: We need to know where problems have come from and where they persist now. And we need to investigate *cooperatively* with the primary goal of identifying problems—this particular behaviour, that particular attitude, this way of speaking, that way of hiring and firing—that we can all tackle *together*.

If CRT helps us to analyze things, then let's hear what it has to say. We must avoid, however, the delicious temptation to fix blame and shame on only certain people, leaving the rest of us nicely unimplicated in what went wrong . . . and therefore implicitly off the hook in doing what now is right. Indeed, we must avoid blaming people for what they themselves didn't do and aren't doing.

Some of us have inherited privileges because of our skin colour, class, sex, and so on. Such realities deserve attention and ownership. Analysis helps us here and we can better engage in such analysis together, benefiting from our diversity. You'll likely see some things I won't, and vice versa.

If I have inherited such privileges, I can then work with you to do something about that, and particularly to obey the Biblical injunctions to right wrongs and to share generously. But I *inherited* those privileges. I can't be blamed for them coming to me. I can be blamed only for exploiting them or for blithely enjoying them without trying to remedy an unjust situation. That's the kernel of truth, I think, in Kendi's anti-racist insistence that if someone like me isn't actively trying to change an inherently unjust situation, I am culpable for acquiescing in it.

The realistic problem that must be faced here paradoxically is brought into focus again by reference to intersectionality. I myself happen to enjoy not just *white* privilege, but also *male* privilege, *class* privilege, the privilege of speaking the world's dominant language, the privilege of elite education, and more. No one can simultaneously be equally concerned about all these realities and equally active in remedying whatever injustices result from them. Hectoring such people for not doing all they can at every moment about everything that's wrong cannot possibly result in sensible, lasting improvement.

Most people don't respond well to accusations of guilt. Most of us, in fact, respond to guilt just enough to quiet guilt feelings. Far better than blame, therefore, is the simple, straightforward analysis of the situation—with the clearly implied *responsibility* to remedy things left to each person's and each society's capacity at that moment to change for the better in that respect. Driven only by guilt feelings, we can expect under- and even sometimes over-reactions. Motivated instead by conscience informed by cooperatively determined responsibility, we ought to pursue healthier possibilities together.

Segmentation instead of community: Discovering that my ancestors oppressed your ancestors may help to explain why we're in the situation we're now in. As a Canadian of primarily English and Scottish descent, I acknowledge that I was born into a bloody heritage.

But who wasn't? And now that we have established what happened, what are we—as *we*—going to do about it? Any champion of DEI and anti-racism who sets this group against that group or this type of person against that type of person is breaking apart what badly needs to be joined together. We must build alliances, not foster rivalries.

It's not as if everyone is equally wrong or responsible, of course. Sometimes a particular group or kind of people really has behaved badly to another, and that's the whole story. Still, social analysis that results in a radical "good guys versus bad guys" situation can't be expected to build much team spirit, and especially when people are commanded to feel guilty for things they themselves didn't do. This is *our* problem, requiring give and take on both sides. The only lasting solutions will be the ones *we* choose.

Complaint instead of justice: If you're in the presence of someone utterly focused on the bad things that have happened instead of the good things that could happen, you're in a dead-end hell of interminable pain. Of course we need to reckon with the past. How did we end up in this horrible hole? Sooner than later, however, we need to focus on finding our way out.

Those who insist on constantly complaining about injustice instead of patiently working for justice merely keep us all moaning and griping in the dark. No one's situation is improved. Such people are the very definition of toxic. Escape them. Find instead the people who aim at creative construction.

Grievance instead of reconciliation: I have had conversations with understandably agitated people with long lists of injuries that I agreed deserve acknowledgement, compassion, and rectification. I've had such talks with First Nations chiefs, Black students, Asian family members, poor neighbours—and women in all of those categories who can testify to intersectionality in heartbreaking detail.

Some of those conversations were agonizing, and they had to be. The good conversations, however (and some of the good ones still hurt), left me thinking that my neighbour wanted to be my neighbour. They weren't just pounding on me as the privileged white Christian man as today's exercise in grievance. They were hoping I could see better what has been wrong and then join with them in making it right. The outcome wasn't endless recrimination but eventual reconciliation. And I was glad to work with them as I could. My friend Irshad Manji runs the Moral Courage Project at Oxford University with the powerfully pithy slogan, "Diversity without Division." Whatever we're going to accomplish we're going to accomplish together.

Christians follow a Lord who was demonstrably committed to diversity, equity, and inclusion. Look at his friends and disciples. Look at his dinner companions. Look at the extended encounters this rabbi had with people who were non-Jewish, non-rich, and non-male. And this Lord preached squarely in the Old Testament prophetic tradition of justice and righteousness in every area of life, toward all of God's creation. Moreover, this Lord never doubted that sin suffuses the structures of power, whether in the Roman Empire, the Jewish monarchy, or the local church (Rev. 2-3).

Christians therefore must pursue justice and compassion alongside our activist neighbours of various ideological stripes insofar as they seek similar outcomes of goodness—especially for the oppressed. Christians therefore must respond to our shouting neighbours with patience, and humility, and compassion, and gentleness, and love. (We do, don't we? We must.) Christians therefore must live lives consistent with the Gospel and converse in ways shaped by the Gospel in hopes that our families and churches and friendships and institutions all evidence this New Life promised by that Gospel.

If Christians will in fact live this way, the Gospel will touch others, as it has from the beginning, and we will see greater justice here and there, by the powerful grace of God. If we Christians do not live this way, well, then, it literally won't matter what we think or say about . . . DEI, CRT, or anything else. So let's think better, yes—and live better.

Deeply complicating this whole conversation, however, is the fog of postmodern doubt and the fragmentation of postmodern differences. Aren't we doomed to seeing things only according to our particular perspectives as largely dictated by our respective communities? How can we hope to see things enough the same way so as to change things enough to gratify everyone's concerns? That's the postmodern situation, and the challenge is daunting.

In the last decade or so, however, something critical has changed in our culture—whether in Australia or Austria. Instead of public and private conversation suffused with the humility of postmodernity—you see it your way, sure, and I see it mine, so let's do what we can to communicate and cooperate—there is instead a new mood of shocking self-confidence. Instead of postmodern modesty, there is instead a post-postmodern stridency. As one wag put it, "I'm right. You're wrong. Go to hell."

In our final two chapters, then, we have to ask, Whatever happened to postmodernity? And why is everyone now shouting?

Chapter Eleven
Postmodernity Revisited

Whatever happened to relativism?

You can still hear preachers say it across North America, throughout the Anglosphere, and likely well beyond. If you're a regular churchgoer, you've doubtless heard it before, and you'll likely hear it again. (I heard it yesterday morning in church.)

"In our culture nowadays," we are solemnly warned, "people feel free to behave as they please. 'Do your own thing!' they say. 'Have it your way!' the commercials tell us. 'You have your reality and I have mine'—say the postmodernists. 'Everything is relative since Einstein'"—and so on.

The invocation of Einstein is what philosophers call a "category mistake." Einstein's theory of relativity has to do with the interchangeability of mass and energy, and not anything to do with morality.

The reference to postmodernity, however, is worth pausing over.

The hippie culture of the late 1960s and 1970s popularized cultural relativism, an idea going back decades through literary and social critic Edward Said to anthropologist Margaret Mead, theologian Ernst Troelstch, and others back into the nineteenth century. Cultural relativism deplored the West's facile moral judgment of other cultures according to Western standards—as if Western standards were simply universal and absolute. Each culture, so it was claimed, stands on its own. The behaviour of people within that culture should be judged only by the standards of that culture.

Such a position would then be radicalized by suggesting that *individuals* are laws unto themselves. "Autonomy" literally means that very thing. So when young people wanted to deviate from the norms of their parents, they could have challenged the regnant conventions and condemned them—as many did. Others, however, took a more peaceable route and asked instead just to be allowed to "live, and let live," "agree to disagree," and, yes, to "do your own thing."

The relevance of postmodernity here appears as we recall one of the key attitudes of the postmodern: doubt about any overarching claims to authority, doubt about any Big Story (what the intellectuals called "metanarratives"), and doubt about any universal standard by which any particular person's ethics could be condemned.

Postmodernists, if they are consistent with this fundamental postmodern mood of doubt, are cultural relativists in the sense that they cannot see any abiding, global categories that transcend every group and every society—or, at least, they cannot see how one could conclusively argue for any set of such categories in a way that justified confident judgment.

Postmodernists, to put it another way, do not disbelieve in so-called absolute truth. There are lots of absolute truths, postmodernists would aver. It's just that we cannot ever be certain about them—beyond statements that philosophers call "analytic" and the rest of us call "truths by definition," such as "all bachelors are unmarried" or "2 + 2 = 4." And we can also be certain about one other class of statements—namely, those about immediate sensations. One cannot be less than certain that one is feeling pain if, in fact, one is feeling pain.

What we might call a *hard* cultural relativism would be rooted in *nihilism*: the conviction that there is no moral direction to the universe, there are no transcendent ethical norms by which everyone and every culture can and ought to be adjudicated. Absent those, therefore, all we have left is this culture and its values, on one hand, and that culture and its values, on the other.

Consistent postmodernists, however, would be *soft* cultural relativists. They would say that no one is in an epistemic position to deny absolute moral truths. What human being could plausibly claim certainty, or even strong confidence, about such a sweeping conclusion?

I suppose one could grant that any individual who deviated from the norms of his or her culture could thus, on postmodern term, be duly criticized. "You aren't observing *our* norms" would be a contextually valid criticism. What happened instead however, is that the postmodern mood of doubt about norms was extended to the radically individual level in order to produce a broad consensus that we can each just "do your own thing, "you do you," "it's all relative," and the like. That's the state at which we have arrived today, say the preachers.

Except—we haven't. That's not what has happened.

Perhaps you have noticed that people nowadays don't sound like postmoderns. Occasionally, sure, people will use such expressions, but, typically, it's just to gently fend off a relative, friend, or even mere acquaintance who presumes to condemn someone else's speech or action. "Hey, now," comes the reply, "let's just live and let live."

No one, however, really believes in cultural relativism when it comes to enormities such as the abuse of children or the torture of pets. No sane person, at least, thinks it's "just different" to murder whom you will, or steal what you like, or lie all the time. People who do hold such values we are strongly inclined to incarcerate in hospitals or prisons as positive dangers, not as mere dissidents. As for immigrants bringing their "cultural practices" to our society, well, we have criminalized female genital mutilation, no matter how "traditional," as we also treat "honour killings," executions for blasphemy or apostasy, and polygamy.

So much, then, for any consistent form of cultural relativism.

The situation today, however, is even less a culture of "do your own thing." We have all seen that social media tends strongly toward moral absolutism, not relativism. We have all seen the popularity, even prevalence, of moral language that is, more precisely, *moralistic*: ethical expressions that are confidently condemning. If being *moral* is holding to ethical norms, being *moralistic* is wagging your finger at other people for not observing those norms. We're talking about a mighty tide of moralism sweeping across our society.

One editorial cartoonist put it succinctly: "I'm right. You're wrong. Go to hell." And people are indeed consigning other people to *social* hell: de-platforming, un-friending, blocking, un-following. Disagree with me enough and I will consign you to social media oblivion. Facebook-wise or Instagram-wise or Whatever-wise, you are dead to me.

What has happened? How did we become such a judgmental culture when the logic of postmodernism should have prompted instead a widespread social humility characterized by a demure reticence about anything even resembling condemnation?

I think we're in a *post*-postmodern situation now. I'm truly sorry about that expression, but for lack of a better one, I think it fits. Or perhaps here is, indeed, a better one: *The New Moralism*. I think we're experiencing a strange resurgence of the Romantic confidence in intuition as the primary guide to life and love.

What is that? And how did we settle on that option?

That's what this chapter will explore. Let's think better about it.

To understand better our current epistemic situation—that is, how we and our contemporaries tend to think nowadays—let's lace up our historical running shoes and sprint through a thousand years of intellectual history. In brief, let's consider in turn the way people in traditional societies sought out knowledge; then moderns; then postmoderns.

Consider a tribal compound or a medieval village. In such traditional societies, gaining knowledge is a matter of *listening back*—listening back to one's elders and to their elders, the ancestors.

All societies change, of course. Traditional societies typically change so slowly and so slightly, however, that tomorrow can be expected to be very much like yesterday. So when one confronts a learning challenge, such as how to care for a horse or how to discipline a child, the intelligent thing to do is to listen to those who have learned the wisdom gained from the long chain of trial-and-error reaching back through the generations: what we can call here *tradition*.

One listens back to one's elders. One does so not because they are smarter than the younger people (they may not be) or wiser or more industrious about knowledge-gathering, or for any reason other than this. The elders are the links to the collective experience and reflection of the group. They pass along what was passed along to them. (*Tradition* comes from a root word that means "to pass along.") And what was passed along to them is what their elders had received from their elders and that they in turn had tested in their own experience.

Honouring tradition isn't mindlessly repeating the words and ideas and ways of the past. It is the appreciative receiving of what has worked: what has proven itself to be true and practical in the lives of those who have gone before.

This process of attending to tradition can be as simple as receiving a family recipe from a grandmother or as complex as a medieval scholar poring over Greek and Latin manuscripts in a dark, drafty library in order to "reconcile the authorities" on a thorny academic question. Traditional societies find knowledge by listening back.

Modern societies listen back, too, but only as a preliminary step. Moderns can (and should) be grateful for the work of their predecessors. Scientist Isaac Newton was the great hero of the Scientific Revolution, in the seventeenth century. He then became the model for the subsequent Enlightenment, in the eighteenth century. The Enlightenment was a cultural movement that, in essence, tried to discover regularities, even "laws," that govern the natural world (chemistry, biology, geology) and even human life (psychology, sociology, politics). Every thinker aimed to become the Newton of his or her discipline. And Newton himself acknowledged that he might see farther than his elders only because he stood on their shoulders.

Most moderns, however—including Sir Isaac himself—weren't usually this modest toward the past. The modern spirit "dared to know" (as philosopher Immanuel Kant put it) by *looking forward*. With all due regard for the work of the ancients, moderns wanted to see and think and know for themselves. And why? Because change was now coming so quickly and at such a scale that the rational thing to do would be to look forward as best we can to anticipate what's coming. Dutifully listening to an elder tell stories around a fire or exposit the Bible in a classroom increasingly made as little sense as asking a typical grandparent to explain to a typical teenager the new apps on the newest cell phone.

Moderns wanted to get out into the world and experience it (the empiricist version of the Enlightenment—think of John Locke) or sit quietly in a chair and think hard about it (the rationalist version of the Enlightenment—think of René Descartes). Having gathered one's data, either from the world of sense experience or the world of introspection (or perhaps both), one then reflected upon this information, formulated conclusions, and then (and this is crucial) set them out in public—what we call *publishing* (think of "public-ing"). The Enlightenment believed in *community* as a crucial element in testing and proving one's ideas.

Thus the Enlightenment fostered not only an increase of research in the universities (which had been started in the middle ages as teaching stations and largely remained such in early modern Europe) but also whole new learned societies. These latter clubs were companies of experts engaged in research and in examining each other's research as it was published in open meetings—open, at least, to anyone qualified in the field—and in the new journals (a word that suggests "today's news") that sprung up to present a steady stream of new research for thoughtful consideration.

The Romantic movement then arose to oppose Enlightenment emphases on analytical dissection and cool abstraction, what the Romantics saw as a "laboratory" or "seminar room" approach to knowledge-seeking. For the Romantics, knowledge was to be found in the countryside, not the city; in the flowering field, not the library; in the intuitions of the heart, not the inferences of the head.

Whereas Isaac Newton the physicist had inspired the Enlightenment, Romantics were poets and painters and composers and historians—and only latterly philosophers. The likes of Wordsworth and Rousseau led the way into big visions of life and complex systems, yes, but also to appreciation of vivid particulars (this flower, that castle, this custom, that nation) rather than bloodless, universal abstractions.

Still, the Romantics shared much with their Enlightenment counterparts. *Both* movements were decidedly *modern*. (Many commentators equate "modernity" simply with the Enlightenment, but this is an important mistake.) Enlightenment and Romantic figures shared the modern inclination to look forward, to perceive and think and conclude for themselves. They shared the modern sense that what each was finding out should be submitted to collective appraisal. Thus Wordsworth sent poems to Shelley and Coleridge, for example, expecting them to receive what he was trying to communicate and expecting them to critique his work on the basis of shared values—not unlike the way a scientist would submit a paper to Britain's Royal Society for judgment.

Above all, Romanticism shared with the Enlightenment a deep confidence that people with the right training and the right temperament and the right motivation could and would progressively explore and understand the truth of things in order to arrive at closer and closer approximations of the truth that all would eventually recognize as such. They might even discover some truths that seemed simply and entirely true (such as Newton's inverse square law of gravitation). Moderns were confident that we are steadily progressing to greater and more accurate apprehensions of reality as it actually is.

It is this confidence that postmoderns have lost.

Modernity undercut people's confidence in traditional authorities—elders, shamans, priests, oracles, scriptures, and rulers. Then postmodernity undercut people's confidence in everything else.

As we have seen, postmodernity, epistemologically speaking, comes down to a mood of pervasive doubt. Jean-François Lyotard's famous phrase is "incredulity toward metanarratives" or, we might say, "doubt about any big stories" (the original French term is *les grands récits*) about the ideologies that purport to describe The Way the World Is.

Such stories could be the story of Christianity, but they could also be the story of the inevitable progress of universal reason (per the Enlightenment), or the story of the upward march of our nation (per Romanticism), or the story of capitalism, or communism, or imperialism, or fascism, or democracy (per the leading ideological options of the twentieth century). Postmoderns look at how so much of the world was exploited and ravaged in the name of one or another of these Grand Narratives, and they grimace in dismay.

So when the next person comes along with his or her Explanation of Everything, postmoderns back away and say, "I doubt it. How could anyone be so sure about such a comprehensive account of everything? How can I be sure your Big Story isn't just a tool of the powerful to justify their privilege and maintain everyone else in subjection?"

In postmodernity, the traditional authorities have already been discredited, but now the modern authorities have been, too. Poets and artists? Talking to themselves about themselves, if they make any sense at all. Philosophers? Hopelessly at odds with each other. Other scholars? Divided into countless little competitive schools. Military or political leaders? Always following secret agenda. Surely we can trust scientists? Well, you hire your Ph.D.'s, and I'll hire mine.

Postmodernity, then, gathers knowledge by *looking around*. Knowledge is whatever you and yours can find in your own circles, according to your own ways of thinking. When Nelson Mandela, the South African leader of resistance to that country's racist doctrine of apartheid, finally got out of prison and came to visit America, New York City hawkers sold T-shirts emblazoned with the postmodern motto, "It's a black thing. You wouldn't understand." If you're Black and from Johannesburg—or Harlem—then you'll get it. Otherwise, you're outside the circle. We have nothing to say to each other if you're *other*.

Again, such deep doubt arose from the traumatic disillusionments of the twentieth century. World War I saw the societies of Europe—societies that seriously believed they were the most advanced cultures the world had ever seen and thus were entitled to bring civilization to the rest of the globe through imperial trade and conquest—go to war. In fact, they savaged each other for five years without any positive outcome for any of the combatants, and instead the destruction of most of the regimes that started the war.

Russia succumbed to communism and then suffered the stupidity, poverty, and megadeaths of Stalinism. Glorious and sophisticated Japan brutalized millions in China and Korea.

The world then endured a global economic disaster a full decade long, only to experience the second half, so to speak, of the first European war now played out in East Asia and the Pacific as well. Postwar postcolonialist euphoria, particularly among the huge populations of Africa and the Indian subcontinent, gave way sooner or later to disillusionment under one or another corrupt regime. After victory in 1949, Mao Zedong went on to impoverish and kill millions of his own people in the name of China's glory, only to be imitated in brutal regimes around the globe. Finally, even the United States, which managed to plow through much of the twentieth century fueled by astounding economic and military growth, lost its confidence under the successive hammer blows of the Vietnam war, the Watergate scandal, the crippling oil crisis, and the debilitating double-digit inflation of the 1970s.

No one escaped radical disillusionment.

Now here's a particularly interesting fact. By the turn of the new millennium, everyone was getting most of their information from a single medium: the internet. And yet everyone knew that it was laughable to believe something just because "I saw it on the internet."

(I pause to appreciate that the internet is primarily a medium and not itself a single source. Yet in our actual experience, I daresay, it functions like a single source. Relatively few people consult other media. And the internet tends to homogenize all sources into its preferred graphic styles, linguistic patterns, and search-engine-optimization protocols. It *feels* like a single source.)

This situation has posed an unparalleled and unendurable epistemological crisis. Never before had a culture relied so heavily on a single access point of knowledge that was at the same time widely acknowledged to be dubious. One couldn't live in a state of perpetual doubt. But that is, in essence, the postmodern condition.

So what was left?

Strictly speaking, nothing was left.

Just let that sink in for a moment—and then we'll see how so many of our neighbours have responded to that intolerable situation.

Chapter Twelve

Christians and the New Moralism

What is a postmodern person to do? How can she possibly live her life in a state of perpetual uncertainty? Maybe the nice man on TV is telling the truth, but maybe not. Maybe that impressive celebrity on that beautifully designed website has the answer, but maybe not. How would one know?

Yet one has to get up in the morning and get about one's day. One has to keep making decisions as if they are not just “true for me” but actually true: decisions about how to raise one’s kids, or what house to buy, or, eventually, pension investments.

The situation, alas, is more acute than that. Living with doubt is difficult, and eventually intolerable. But it is simply impossible in crisis. And many North Americans, as is true of people elsewhere, of course, feel themselves to be in crisis.

Economically, many people have not only lost their jobs, but they have no hope of finding another similar job. Some jobs have disappeared to other regions and countries. Other jobs have disappeared because of increased automation. To loss, therefore, is added the crushing burden of despair.

To this economic stress is added the ethical stress of living in a rapidly pluralizing society in which values previously taken for granted are openly flouted. Whether it is alt-right racists on the streets or the militant activist burning down the store his own father built, the majority not on either extreme shake their heads at the loss of a moral consensus and the arrival of what can seem like ethical anarchy—a danger especially, they feel, to their children. When the political choices arise, therefore, these embattled folk don't feel much like compromise. In fact, compromise seems like collusion with, even capitulation to, an enemy: an economic enemy, an ethnic enemy, an *ethical* enemy.

America itself—or Canada, or Britain, or Australia—can seem to be under attack from without and within. Responding to attack requires action. Action requires conviction. And conviction cannot emerge from pervasive postmodern doubt.

Many people in our time, therefore, have fallen back on their own experience and judgment, to what seems to them just obviously true and good. More and more people—our so-called *post*-postmoderns—thus have resorted to *intuition* as their guide to knowledge. What is right—both true and good—is whatever seems simply evident to me as right. My attitude toward vaccination, my vote in an election, my diet, my ethic: it is finally up to me, so I will decide based on what I believe, on what I think I know plus what I value. From *listening-back* to *looking-forward* to *looking-around* we have come to *looking-within*—but critically, without necessarily any introspection.

Consumerism is that attitude toward life fostered by endless advertisements that picture each of us as a little sovereign, self—choosing freely among, say, breakfast cereals without regard to anyone or anything else. And consumerism has now become a general epistemological stance. What is true is whatever seems *to me* to be true. What if I find that experts and major institutions disagree with me? Too bad. As a sovereign self who has gotten postmodernly wise to the duplicity of elites, I'll make up my own mind, thank-you. Our culture therefore endures the endless shouting, sloganeering, and oversimplification of social media in which everyone is confidently, even aggressively, right.

Moreover, everyone finds likeminded people to confirm our views as we harden our minds against alternatives. And the internet has facilitated the hardening of opinions by the reinforcement of group solidarity in several key ways:

• *accessibility*: People who had unusual opinions normally faced steady, silent social pressure to keep such views to themselves. The internet, however, makes allies "find-able" among the vast numbers of people online.

• *secrecy*: Minority views become "say-able" in the private pockets of the internet, and then they are confirmed by the agreement and encouragement of others. What was previously unsayable, almost unthinkable, becomes increasingly just *right*.

• *publicity*: Once my allies and I are convinced we are right and that our opinion must be voiced to help save the nation, the internet that allowed us to be both connected and covert now grants us a public megaphone. Gone are the days when one could address a significant public only by conforming with the editorial policies of a relatively few media outlets. Now, thanks to social media, anyone can say almost anything in public.

• *reinforcement*: Having said what we want to say, if the "likes" come our way, then algorithmic selectivity boosts our signal—especially to like-minded folk. Now what was once not even voiced becomes a viable public option with de facto authority.

To an outside observer, this situation may resemble the Sixties slogan of "Do your own thing," but I hope it's clear now that it really isn't relativism—the conviction that all judgments of truth, goodness, and beauty must be made relative to a particular culture's values since there is no absolute standard. If anyone *ever* truly thought this way, who does nowadays?

Nowadays, instead, we have person after person and group after group making it quite clear to themselves and to anyone who will listen that they are simply and entirely right and everyone who disagrees is simply and entirely wrong. Not *different*: wrong. This is a kind of neo-Romanticism, this resurgence of confidence in intuition: what simply seems right. It certainly lacks the sophistication of a Lake Poet or the polymathic genius of a Jean-Jacques Rousseau. But it's increasingly the norm—the loud, insistent norm—of social media, private life, and, increasingly, public life as well.

The situation is positively poisonous. Indeed, it's worse than I've been saying. If the other side of any debate were in truth merely wrong, we could argue with them—you know, like we did in olden days: adduce evidence, reason carefully and transparently, and trust that people of adequate intelligence and goodwill would either agree with us or point out problems in our thinking that would help everyone get closer to the truth.

Like in a science lab.

Like in a graduate school seminar.

Like in a good professional conference or business meeting.

And now?

Now, well, if you don't agree with me, perhaps it's because you're not quite bright enough. So, if I'm in an expansive mood, I'll explain it to you again, although I'll talk slower and use simpler words.

Still don't agree? My only conclusion is that you are either helplessly stupid (you *can't* see it) or hopelessly wicked (you *won't* see it). Either way, we're done. I'm right. You're wrong. There's no point discussing it further. That's that. And if you persist in your stupid or wicked ways, the only prudent thing to do (and here's where good, helpful psychology gets mixed into the situation in a bad, harmful way) is for me to avoid such toxic people, such as you have proven yourself to be. So I will cut you out of my life.

At the social level of organizations, the only prudent thing to do also is to avoid toxic people. So now we won't allow them even to speak on our university campuses, or make suggestions at our shareholders' meetings, or articulate alternative opinions in our mass media. Why expose ourselves, and vulnerable others, to what is patently, obviously, intuitively wrong? And if all the other right-thinking people think the way we do, why expose ourselves to the financial risk of cancelation by our own patrons for giving a platform to wicked falsehood?

In the New Moralism we face people who are completely convinced of the correctness and importance of their views. Many of those people, moreover, believe they are under threat, or have already been attacked, by cultural and social forces intent on replacing their preferred way of life with something very different.

Certainty + Importance + Conflict = Warfare.

Compromise with enemies in a culture war is impossible. Conversation with the devil is impossible. Only conquest will do, and if I cannot conquer you by persuasion, I will have to conquer you by force: by voices, by votes, by dollars, by policies, and by laws. There remains now only yes or no, right or wrong, with us or against us.

People are sounding like, because they are feeling that, they are at war. Living with, let alone informing and persuading, such people will require us to empathize with their sense of being under siege. Writing them off as paranoid or pathetically self-pitying means the end of our common life.

So how are we to communicate across these divides—or, perhaps better, through these slammed and locked doors? How, in particular, can Christians possibly share the gospel, our own metanarrative that we truly think is the Good News for Everyone?

We can use the various techniques of mediation to try gently to open people up to alternatives. We can ask questions—Why do you think that? How do you know that? What are you most afraid of? What do you most hope for? We can tell stories—anecdotal or historical—to enter some alternative narratives into the record. We can cite sources respected by both sides—such as the Bible, for Christians—in hopes that both sides will be open to correction from a mutually acknowledged authority. In any given case, such measured overtures might initiate genuine conversation.

Each of these suggestions deserve extended discussion and application. For now, however, let's focus on one key word: *authenticity*. No word means more to people nowadays than that. "Natural" used to be the best word to use in marketing, but we all now realize how plastic (so to speak) that word can be. *Authentic* has the ring of, well, reality. And confident apprehension of reality is, in these postmodern times, a prize everyone values.

How, then, to offer the Gospel—truly a metanarrative, the Big Story That Explains All Other Stories—to a wary world? How, then, to offer the Gospel in a culture in which most people still think they understand Christianity and have made their minds up about Christianity while (poll after poll clearly demonstrates) they really don't have even the basics of Christianity—Trinity, Incarnation, Atonement—clearly in mind?

If in doubt (and who isn't, in postmodernity?), ask the Lord. And here is what the Lord says: "Let your light shine before others, that they may see your good deeds and glorify your Father in heaven" (Matthew 5:16).

And the Apostle Peter: "Live such good lives among the pagans that, though they accuse you of doing wrong, they may see your good deeds and glorify God on the day he visits us" (1 Peter 2:12).

And the Apostle Paul: "Good deeds are obvious, and even those that are not obvious cannot remain hidden forever" (1 Timothy 5:25).

Jesus and his followers lived in a culture unkindly disposed toward Christianity. The idea at the very heart of Christianity—that God was incarnate in Christ, who suffered, died, and rose again to save the world—was foolishness to the best of Gentile civilization ("How can the Eternal become mortal? That's ridiculous") and repellent to the Israelites ("How can God Almighty become a man who dies? That's disgusting"). Even someone with the intellect of the Apostle Paul could barely make a dent in the adamantine resistance of clever Greeks and learned Jews.

Preach on, they did. Jesus did. Peter did. Paul did—despite resistance, scorn, indifference, yes, but also beatings, whippings, and imprisonment, ending in execution.

What they recommended to their fellow Christians as a pattern of life functioning as a form of witness, however, was primarily that of quiet lives well-lived and characterized by good works indisputable to their fellow citizens. Even the infamous emperor Julian the Apostate, who tried to roll back the Christian tide following Constantine in the fourth century, was dismayed at good works—among Jews and even more among the Christians, whom he called "impious Galileans." They shamed good pagans such as himself. He ordered Arsacius, his high priest of the region of

Galatia, "to build in each city frequent hostels in order that strangers may profit by our philanthropy; I do not mean for our own people only, but for others also who are in need of money. . . . For it is disgraceful that, when no Jew ever has to beg, and the impious Galileans support not only their own poor but ours as well, all men see our people lack aid from us."

The Salvation Army, World Vision, A Rocha, the Christian overnight shelter, your local church's food bank—these speak volumes. Indeed, in India today, Christian good works are so plentiful that Hindu activists feel obliged to disparage them. They commonly excoriate acts of Christian charity as mere "inducements" to convert—as if Christians were spending all this time, energy, and money to make converts who will—what? Merely replace some of that time, energy, and money, in the dumbest Ponzi scheme in the world?

Yes, there are still other ways of commending the great truths of the gospel in our post-modernly resistant and post-postmodernly dogmatic age. Comedy, perhaps, and well-crafted songs, and thoughtful screenplays, and provocative pictures all alluding and even occasionally referring to Christ and the Bible while not tripping the circuit-breakers of our over-sensitive neighbours. We need to encourage the talented artists in our circles to speak the truth as they can to those they alone can reach.

Some of us can and must speak up—in our families, schools, workplaces, and public forums—on behalf of liberal values that are essential to the wellbeing of the Church and its proclamation, as well as to that of society at large. Churches can and should support religious freedom for all. We need to call both our fellow Christians and also our fellow citizens to defend fully and consistently human rights *for everyone*, including sexual and ethnic minorities, yes, but also including Christians. There should be no double standards favouring or discriminating against anyone sincerely trying to abide by the rules of our common life.

In Canada, we experience two conspicuous double standards these days. Christianity comes in for extra criticism, if not outright contempt, while aboriginal folkways enjoy elite interest and even promotion. In official ceremonies, for instance, whether at university graduations or public holiday gatherings, a Christian prayer offered by a Christian clergyperson—positively *expected* in Canadian public life just a generation ago—would likely now come under heavy fire. Meanwhile, a First Nations prayer, preferably offered by a chief or shaman in full regalia, would be welcomed.

As a Christian who has taught the history of settler/aboriginal relations as part of the history of religion in Canada, I frankly think both double standards are wrong. But they are also quite understandable and almost certainly temporary. We Christians used to run Canada and we made some terrible mistakes along the way, particularly toward minorities who didn't conform to our expectations. No wonder lots of Canadians don't like our religion, our churches, or us. We may well have to simply endure the resentment of "the sins of the fathers" being visited on the next generation or so. Meanwhile, it's not as if native Canadians all enjoy a sunny life these days. Consider the brutal fact that many reserves across this water-rich country don't have a reliable supply of clean water—in the 2020s. So I'm prepared to gently object, when I can, to discrimination against Christians, while I'm also prepared to press our elites to go beyond public gestures of goodwill toward First Nations to actually resolving land claims, finding ways to save their young people from epidemic rates of suicide, and, yes, getting them all some clean water.

I recognize that the history of Black slavery in the United States continues to dominate the social consciousness of that great land, often overshadowing the pressing legitimate concerns of Latinos and native Americans, among others. The United Kingdom's internecine warfare over Brexit has prompted racial and other tensions to surface in disturbing ways. And

Australians and New Zealanders—different as those two countries have been in their relations with aboriginal populations—continue to struggle toward healthy, sustained, and productive accommodation of their differences, including their different hurts from their different histories. In order to bless our fractious societies and particularly to care for those still less powerful than ourselves, Christians ought to be the first to compromise our privileges and, in extreme cases, even our rights—as Paul says the correctly charitable use of Christian liberty requires, and as he himself did on occasion as a Roman citizen.

We should note also, however, that Paul did sometimes invoke that Roman citizenship. So should we Christians properly resist any curtailment of our freedom especially to live and speak on behalf of the gospel. This is what it means to be genuinely tolerant and genuinely principled, with sufficient attendant self-examination that we know when we're actually in danger versus simply uncomfortable.

We therefore can judiciously endorse CRT and DEI and anti-racism and political correctness *when they properly target actual wrongs and proceed to make things better*. Woke culture isn't wrong about everything!

Woke culture isn't right about everything, though, either. Christians must reserve the right to criticize, demur from, and even oppose anyone who would impose his or her values on the rest of us in the name of righteousness. There must be room for dissent, both creative and critical, or human beings are being prevented from enjoying their God-given rights. We must all be liberals in this sense, defending maximal freedom and respectful toleration for everyone—not just ourselves and those who agree with us

Furthermore, no one but Jesus deserves blanket endorsement, not even the Church—let alone our favourite political party or leader. Woke culture, like any other package of human aspirations and concerns, is truly *human*:

both imaging God in some way and suffused with evil in some way. It is thus both honourable in much of its intention while vulnerable also to searching critique. Thoughtful Christians therefore should neither accept nor reject it *in toto*, as we should neither accept nor reject anything *in toto* except the Lord Jesus and his Word.

Some of us, therefore, have the artistic ability to get through to some of our neighbours who would be open to hints of God's light, however quickly they would repel any direct approach with the gospel. Others of us have the verbal ability to get through to some of our neighbours who would be open to arguments based on our common liberal values, however indifferent to those values so many seem to be today.

What *each* of us can do is what the New Testament says to do: build authentic Christian communities, especially churches and families, and simply live accordingly.

And when some, at least, ask about the hope that motivates you—as some will, particularly as crises come, as crises do—we can and must be prepared to explain the good news about the Person at the heart of it all (1 Peter 3:15). Even then, Peter goes on to say, keep "a clear conscience, so that those who speak maliciously against your good behavior in Christ may be ashamed of their slander"—as those foolish BJP types in India today are going to be recognized in due course as murderously ridiculous for persecuting Christians, just as the late Christopher Hitchens was humiliated by his ugly and idiotic attacks on Mother Teresa.

Lots of people know the good when they see it. And our good news, after all, is about the Good Person at the centre of the Good Life. May God help us live such good lives that some people—drawn by God, to be sure—will ask us about the Source of that goodness. For if we don't, they won't.

But if we do, they will. And what a Story we'll have for them then.

Afterword

I'm writing this book in Canada as a Canadian, even as I'm delighted to address friends in other countries. At the time of this writing, our Canadian prime minister is Justin Trudeau, leader of the Liberal Party. And he is "liberal" in most senses of that word.

In fact, our prime minister could rightly be called "woke." That, at least, is the consensus of pundits at home and abroad. *The Globe and Mail,* Canada's answer to *The New York Times,* sees him in the vanguard of the "Woke Generation," while the *Times* of London pronounces him "the Wizard of Woke."

Mr. Trudeau does seem to be woke indeed. He is manifestly, even assertively, alert to at least certain questions of injustice, especially regarding gender, sex, and race. He also leads the way on particular issues of individual autonomy—from abortion to MAiD ("medical assistance in dying"), and from legal use of marijuana to the state support of sex and gender transitions. Mr. Trudeau's apparently unshakeable confidence in the intuitive goodness of his values and policies can exasperate some. Others cringe at what can seem to be his heavy-handed performance of virtue—perhaps inescapable in politics, but unseemly nonetheless. Still, these traits are not ingredient to "wokeness." What makes him truly woke is his embrace of a particular flavour of progressive politics.

As I detailed in the introduction, the term "woke" goes back decades, to the question of whether Americans were willing to acknowledge the systemic patterns of racial discrimination evident well after the Civil War. Critical Race Theory is only the most recent attempt to wake people up to the injustices intrinsic to the interlocking legal, political, economic, and cultural systems of the United States—and beyond.

Here in Canada, we have Black/white problems of our own, of course. We also confront painful questions surrounding First Nations and settlers, citizens and immigrants, men and women, the one per cent and the rest of us, and more. To be aware of these problems and to be willing to face them is to be legitimately woke. In that sense, we are all woke now—or, at least, our mainstream media, party politicians, and even major corporations keep these issues in the forefront of Canadian public conversation.

I recall, however, Søren Kierkegaard's call to his fellow nineteenth-century Danes to wake up out of their sleepwalking formal "Christianity" to begin a truly vital walk with God. I recall Blaise Pascal's seventeenth-century observation that we middle-class types spend a lot of resources keeping ourselves in spiritual somnolence, gently insulated from disturbing questions of the meaning of life and what lies beyond the grave. And, in between those two great thinkers, I recall that when the gospel was preached by George Whitefield in the American colonies of the eighteenth century, it touched off, yes, the Great *Awakening*. Is Canada fully woke by those measures? Is America? The United Kingdom? Australia? New Zealand?

We Canadians are more aware than ever before of injustices to many, perhaps most, of our people not identified with the two "founding" nations of French and English Christians—from First Nations to East Asians to South Asians to Jews to Muslims. Canada has taken great strides to care better for the needs of disabled people, mentally ill people, and poor people. We treat more fairly than we did our young people, old people, and, yes, female and non-gender-conforming people. All of these developments, all of this "wokeness," warrants Christian support and celebration. Similar strides have been taken in other Western countries.

A fearsome narrowing of human aspirations to material comfort, economic security, ecological gentleness, and moral license, however, is evident. Consider the change over the last generation or so in the student choice of majors at universities. Consider the party platforms and spending priorities of governments. These narrowed values bespeak an obtuse unawareness of both the deep spiritual pathology of humanity and the dazzling range of human potential in all of us as depicted in the Bible.

Evangelical Christians typically have helped to wake up societies to injustice and need. Sunday schools, temperance movements, abolitionism, female suffrage, hospitals, adoption agencies—our heritage is full of initiatives at the cutting edge of "wokeness." Let us be careful, therefore, not to abandon that zeal for social reform just because others attempt it in ways we cannot fully endorse and, in some cases, might even have to resist.

Let me say that again. Just because some people in our society pursue only certain good ends while pursuing others we detest, just because some people try to attach bad agenda to good, and just because some people over-react and over-correct in their zeal doesn't mean we should wash our hands of the whole matter, let alone mount campaigns against all things woke. Social change, until the Lord returns, will always be messy: piecemeal, erratic, mixed, disappointing. Our calling, however, is to make things better. We can't make them perfect, since only the Lord himself can do that. Politics is the art of the possible. So let us not be weary in well-doing, but instead let us make what alliances we can to make what progress we can. We thus will be like our Father in heaven, who blesses everyone trying to make shalom (Matthew 5:9), sending rain to nurture the righteous and unrighteous alike (Matthew 5:45).

Let us also, however, renew our zeal for our particular Christian calling to tell the Big Story of the Bible, the Story of the disaster of sin and of the divine exertions necessary to remedy it, the Big Story of the original potential of our world and the glorious hope of the world to come. Let us build churches that teach this bigger, better view of things, vital communities that demonstrate a bigger, better life, spiritual families that issue bigger, better invitations to our neighbours to come join us—to become, indeed, fully awake.

About the Author

Front-line academic research grounds John Stackhouse's work. He draws together both information and patterns from several disciplines to inform and equip individuals and organizations to succeed.

Holding a Ph.D. in history and theology from The University of Chicago, he has published a dozen books and lectures at universities around the world.

His work has been featured by many media, such as *The New York Times*, *The Washington Post*, and *The Times Literary Supplement*. He has appeared on national television and radio networks in the United States, Canada, and Australia.

Professor Stackhouse has addressed audiences as varied as the Young Presidents Organization, the Kirby Laing Centre at Cambridge University, the Christian Medical and Dental Society, the Conservative Party of Canada, InterVarsity Christian Fellowship, Christians for Biblical Equality, and the Alberta Teachers Association.

He has also rendered expert testimony to the British Columbia Supreme Court, the Manitoba Human Rights Commission, and the Canada Revenue Agency. He is a sought-after consultant with CEOs, physicians, industry leaders, pastors, lawyers, and politicians around the globe on culture, strategy, and ethics.

https://facebook.com/ProfStackhouse

https://twitter.com/jgsphd

https://instagram.com/prof_john_stackhouse

THINKBETTER Media

Equipping leaders and earnest disciples with Christian ethics to navigate crucial issues in contemporary culture.

Ministry & Discipleship Resources

Accessible resources on complex subjects, broken down into specific, concrete, and practical content.

- Signature Series: Short articles series present sustained analysis and critical evaluations of crucial issues and their implications for your life and work.
- Seminar Videos: Recorded presentations offer context and clarity with practical take-aways in conversation with other highly motivated participants..
- Live Webinars: Interactive learning with opportunity to share your own ideas, ask your particular questions, and get advice about your urgent challenges.
- Resource Library: Our online multimedia library contains all our Signature Series, seminar videos, live webinars, expert interviews, discussion guides, and hundreds of catalogued blog posts.. And we're growing it every month!

Check out these resources and more at thinkbettermedia.ca

THINKBETTER Media

Equipping leaders and earnest disciples with Christian ethics to navigate crucial issues in contemporary culture.

Seminars & Consulting

Hands-on group training or private consulting to help leaders and organizations with the challenges facing you in contemporary culture.

Work with Prof. John Stackhouse to get—

(1) **Clarity:** analysis of your pressing situation based on the best social science, philosophy, and theology and expressed in accessible and compelling terms;

(2) **Context:** a vivid understanding of the genesis of your challenge—your story, the story of your organization, and the story of your context; and

(3) **Actionables:** concrete recommendations for the real world from an award-winning ethicist, expert legal witness, and experienced institutional consultant.

For seminar booking or speaking requests please contact thinkbetter@johnstackhouse.com